HAPPINESS:
A MATTER OF PERSPECTIVE

Everything in the universe is always changing and everything is dependent on everything else.

*Hidden or manifest
is a matter of perspective.*

HAPPINESS:
A MATTER OF PERSPECTIVE

Thich Vien Ngo

Translated by Ton That Chieu, MD
Dharma name: Tam Hien

Printed at Focus Digital Publishing, in Virginia - 2022

Copyright © 2021 by Thich Vien Ngo
All rights reserved.

ISBN 978-168564108-5

Contents

Contents 6
INTRODUCTION 8
ORIGINAL PUBLISHER'S FOREWORD 10
AUTHOR'S PREFACE 13
LIST OF ABBREVIATIONS 15
RECOGNIZING SUFFERING TO REDUCE SUFFERING 16
HAPPINESS: A MATTER OF PERSPECTIVE 21
SKILLFUL HANDS 25
THE BEAUTY OF DAWN 29
HAPPINESS IS MUTUAL ACCEPTANCE 33
FLOWERS AND GARBAGE 37
BREATHING: A BODY-MIND THERAPY 41
HAPPINESS IS MANIFEST 45
MOTHER'S ADVICE 49
GRATITUDE 52
SPRING IS HERE 55
THE ART OF TEA DRINKING 59
LISTENING DEEPLY TO PROMOTE HAPPINESS 62
SELF-TRANSFORMATION TO FULFILL FILIAL PIETY 66
INTROSPECTION GENERATES COMPASSION 70
TAKING REFUGE IN THE DHARMA 73
SHARING CONFIDENCES WITH A NOVICE MONASTIC 77
THE TEACHER-STUDENT BOND 80
WISDOM IS SHINING 85

DEEP LISTENING, THOROUGH UNDERSTANDING AND GREAT LOVE	89
WHOLE-HEARTED REPENTANCE	94
TAKING REFUGE IN THE THREE JEWELS	99
NO TIME FOR DHARMA PRACTICE	103
SEEING CLEARLY THE ILLUSORY SELF	108
LOOKING FOR OBJECTS OF LOVE AND COMPASSION	113
LEARNING DHARMA WITH AN OPEN MIND	117
NO BLAME TO ANYONE	121
AS KIND AS A BUDDHA	126
HONORING THE BUDDHA	130
AWARENESS OF BODY AND MIND	135
INSIGHT AND INNER CALM	140
BEING KIND TO EACH OTHER	145
IN ACCORD WITH IMPERMANENCE	149
FAMILY LEGACY	153
THE BEAUTY OF ANGER	157
STAYING CAREFREE WHILE HAVING ATTACHMENTS	161
TWO ASPECTS OF LIFE	165
COME AND SEE	170
Afterword by Dr. Mylene Tran Huynh	175
Translator's Note	178
Glossary	180
Comments on HAPPINESS: A MATTER OF PERSPECTIVE	182
About the Author	183

INTRODUCTION
by Venerable Vien Minh

Whenever we met, I have been impressed by Bhikkhu Thich Vien Ngo's enthusiastic study and practice of the Dharma. I was even more impressed when I read his book *Happiness: A matter of perspective*, in which he shares his Buddhist knowledge.

Unlike books by intellectual Bhikkhus, his writings originate from his life experiences and his own understanding, rather than through just translating the literal meaning of the sutras. Truth is not reserved for monastics in monasteries or temples. It is also not the monopoly of any famous master. Truth is that which is in accord with facts, reality (*sandittiko*). Everyone can see the truth anywhere and anytime if their eyes are not clouded by dust. Truth is not formed by concepts, formulas, methods, or sectarian doctrines. The unique contribution of the Buddha is to reveal Truth to human beings: to attain enlightenment is the task of each practitioner. Each person must live through, contemplate, and apply his own experiences in order to discover and realize the truth in his own life. Truth is an absolute perfection, but the means and methods of transmitting Truth are relative and imperfect. The difficulty for the practitioner is that he must clearly see and experience for himself in order to adapt to circumstances and to avoid stereotypes and obsolete formulas. Truth remains the same, but its application is forever evolving. We best not cling to any conclusion or any affirmation in order to go with the flow of life's conditions and ever-changing phenomena. (*Svakhato Baghavata Dhammo*).

Each individual finds solutions for his problems in different ways depending on his background, identity, lifestyle, and karma. An awakened person only helps others find the correct direction in order to adjust their thoughts and actions to particular situations. The awakened person does not offer any definitive solution. For example, a student solves a mathematical problem according to his level, but the teacher cannot help him at the teacher's own level of education and experience. Of course, the student will reach a better solution after entering a higher grade. The same situation applies to a Buddhist practitioner who may improve his thoughts and actions without following any ideal model. This is because a correct solution at one time and in one place may become wrong at another time and place.

I hope that the sincere suggestions from Bhikkhu Thich Vien Ngo will serve as typical examples enabling all people to find solutions for their own problems in this life of "True Emptiness, Wonderful Existence."

Most Venerable Vien Minh

Buu Long Patriarchal Hall, District 9, HCM City, Saigon

ORIGINAL PUBLISHER'S FOREWORD

Two years ago, I received a gift from Bhikkhu Thich Vien Ngo. It was his book *Happiness*, and I devoured it that first night. As I read the book, I had the impression he was writing about my own thoughts. Silently, I thanked him.

The earth meanwhile spins and orbits around the sun. Days and nights pass. Spring comes, then summer, followed by autumn and winter. A year later, I reread the book, at the end of the year 2013, and talked with the Board of the publishing company about reprinting the 2nd edition. After their approval, I informed Bhikkhu Thich Vien Ngo and fortunately he concurred with the decision.

The earth is covered by a layer of air like a blanket for human beings in winter. However, this blanket always changes form, inflated on one side and deflated on the other. Like the blanket covering the earth, we are covered and protected by loving-kindness all around us, from the father-sun and mother-earth. The inflated and deflated side is simply a matter of our perspective about what is happening in our daily life. The way we see it is who we are. This is a real wonder, indeed.

As I write this, I remember how some of my friends have thought that I am "naive." This was during the second time that I left Hanoi on Lunar New Year (Tet) to go to Saigon for the one-week Road Book Festival. The Board of Directors and executive officer of the publisher previously felt pity for me as I left FPT (a famous electronic company in Hanoi, Vietnam) to form Thai Ha Publishing Company. They felt that most people would rather watch TV than read a book. Friends at the Publishing Company also told me that I was doubly naive because I published books about education, Buddhism, and living according to the Buddhist ethics of karma. These books are usually published for donation and not for sale. I was startled and told myself that although they thought I was an idiot, I consider myself a wise man. The businesspeople who told me so are, as an old Vietnamese expression puts it, "wealthy but owning nothing" while I and my colleagues at Thai Ha Book are truly rich. The businesspeople are rich in terms of money and material possessions, while we have love, understanding and wisdom. We are happy every day. In every moment in life. Editing, proofreading, designing, typography, pre-press, printing, publishing, and marketing. We are rich without being noticed.

Since *Happiness: A Matter of Perspective* was first published in 2012, the author added fourteen chapters for this new edition. Thus, the perspective of the readers becomes wider and their happiness greater. I want you to read it slowly. Think about it so it can transform your view.

I will be deeply sorry if after reading this book, you are not happy. If that is the case, then I and Bhikkhu Thich Vien Ngo would like to invite you to a conversation.

Sometimes, I imagine myself standing on the peak of the Himalaya mountains looking down at the earth, seeing all sentient beings, and contemplating animals, plants, mountains, rivers, grass and sand. Before the wonders of nature, I feel extremely happy. Yesterday, I was also incredibly happy when I looked at a one-year-old child who walked slowly with a beautiful smile. My body and mind were immersed in happiness.

As such, I wanted to expand my feeling and perspective to my co-workers and to everybody.

I am aware that now, many people are addicted to alcohol. Others are "killing time" in unhealthy games and gambling. Some are obsessed by negative thoughts, which may cause harm to themselves, their loved ones and the community. Therefore, I hope this book not only benefits businessmen and intellectuals, but also the underprivileged. We may print more copies as gifts to them, or even have it read to them. This certainly will transform their mind. Happiness is not only enjoying but also sharing and giving.

I send my congratulations to you because you already have this valuable book. Your next step is to read, deeply understand, and enjoy it. Please give it a big smile.

Nguyễn Mạnh Hùng, Ph.D.

President, Thái Hà Books

AUTHOR'S PREFACE

Happiness: A matter of perspective is a collection of my writings which have appeared in the Buddhism section of the weekly magazine *Giác Ngộ* (Enlightenment), published in Vietnam. Most of these texts include excerpts from the Nikaya and Agamma Sutras; all these texts are based on the Buddha's essential teachings and on my own experiences in Dharma practice.

I hope to help beginners learn and practice Buddhism in order to overcome and transform the obstacles and suffering of daily life. With a deep aspiration to propagate the Buddha Dharma to benefit all beings, and despite my humble knowledge of Buddhism, I have tried my best to apply my knowledge and experience towards cultivating and transmitting the Dharma. This is also my modest contribution to the noble task of the Patriarchs and great Dharma Masters.

To varying degrees, human beings encounter difficulties and obstacles in life. However, happiness or suffering depends on each individual's perspective. If we live with mindfulness in the present moment, we can remain calm and peaceful despite unwanted circumstances.

I have put my best efforts and reflections into this work in order to bring joy and benefit to its readers. Due to my limitations, I can share only some aspects of daily life, nor have I elaborated on all the profound passages excerpted from various sutras. I hope to receive comments from readers and venerable Dharma Masters.

Namo Sakyamuni Buddha

Phước Viên Temple, Biên Hòa, Đồng Nai, Việt Nam

Thich Viên Ngộ

LIST OF ABBREVIATIONS

AN: Anguttara Nikaya

DN: Digha Nikaya

IT: Itivuttaka

MN: Majjihima Nikaya

PTS: Pali Text Society

SN: Samyutta Nikaya

RECOGNIZING SUFFERING TO REDUCE SUFFERING

To a certain degree, everybody in the world undergoes some kind of suffering in life. We suffer when our body hurts; anger causes suffering; regret also creates suffering. There are many sources of suffering, but, in the end, they all derive from ourselves.

Suffering is an obvious truth; no one can deny it. This is the first of the four Noble Truths in Buddhism. Anywhere in this world, even when we have money, education, prestige, or power, we are still dominated by suffering. So long as we do not recognize and transform the seeds of anger, greed, sadness, anxiety, fear, jealousy, and blame in our body and mind, it is easy for us to be bound and chained by these afflictions. However, the possibility of happiness, or the absence of suffering, is the second Noble Truth. If, right in this moment, we see clearly each event happening in our mind and our surrounding circumstances with an honest, clear, objective, state of mind, then suffering does not have the opportunity to manifest. In the Satipatthana Sutra, the Buddha taught:

"Here, Bhikkhus, a bhikkhu dwells perceiving again and again the body as just the body, with diligence, clear understanding and mindfulness, thus keeping away the covetousness and mental pain in the world; he dwells perceiving again and again the feelings as just the feelings, with diligence, clear understanding and mindfulness, thus

keeping away the covetousness and mental pain in the world; he dwells perceiving again and again the mind as just the mind, with diligence, clear understanding and mindfulness, thus keeping away the covetousness and mental pain in the world; he dwells perceiving again and again the Dharmas as just the Dharmas, with diligence, clear understanding (awareness) and mindfulness, thus keeping away the covetousness and mental pain in the world." (MN: Vol. I).

The diligence mentioned in the above sutra is not the effort of a greedy ego. It only requires us to invest our attention in closely observing objective reality. Mindfulness means we do not forget reality or else we will be swayed by outside circumstances. Instead, we must always return to ourselves. Awareness means a clear, honest, objective view, unclouded by the maneuvers of consciousness or subjective thought.

Therefore, having diligence, awareness, and mindfulness to keep away worldly covetousness means that we only need to understand what is happening in our body and mind in the present situation and be fully present with it. We must recognize the present situation as it is and not add or subtract from it. Thus, we will not be bound by the Three Poisons, as identified by Buddha: greed, anger and ignorance.

Suffering begins with a mind that is either clinging to or averse to its object. On the contrary, when we get in touch with any situation and merely recognize it without covetousness or aversion, suffering will not have the basis for arising. Our true illness is coveting pleasant objects for the satisfaction of our senses and opposing or running away from we do not like. There is the cause of affliction and suffering. When we expect to attain anything, the greedy mind arises.

When we dream of achieving something but fail, we will surely suffer (not getting what one desires is suffering); when we try to exclude what is unpleasant to us, the angry mind arises (coming into contact with the undesired is suffering), and if we want to but we are unable to abolish what is unpleasant, the suffering is even more intense. When we encounter unpleasant circumstances in daily life in this way, we will thus be immersed in suffering and instability.

Human beings are bound by suffering because we do not recognize how consciousness arises and operates. In fact, when sorrow emerges in our mind, we only need to see it clearly; calling it by its true name is enough: Hello, my friend Sadness, how are you? Please sit down and drink tea with me. Or when anger arises, we also call it by its true name: Hi, my dear friend Anger, are you trying to find me? Just like that, if we welcome our suffering joyfully, we have nothing to worry about. And when we co-exist peacefully and cheerfully with our suffering, and interact appropriately with it, there will be nothing unpleasant for us to fear or run away from.

A good example of this realization can be found in the story about a soldier returning to his village after the war. During the war, the soldier had spent days and nights climbing mountains, wading streams, and crossing forests, encountering numerous, great hardships. He ate uncooked meals, drank untreated river water, slept in the wilderness, spent days in rain and bad weather, never knowing when he might die by gunfire or bombs. After the war was over, he could return home to live peacefully in his village. Even if he occasionally encountered economic difficulty, it was nothing compared to the times when he was still in the battlefield facing immeasurable suffering. So suffering is not always the terrible thing that we must avoid, but it may rather be a teacher for us to realize the true value of our life. It is just like the lotus flower: it becomes beautiful and fragrant because it co-exists with the dirty, foul-smelling mud; without mud, how can there be lotus flowers? Therefore, mud is essential for lotus plants to produce fresh, lovely flowers as gifts to the world.

    Reacting to and resisting objects of mind are due to the intervention of our ego. Such phenomena, also called dharmas, always operate according to the law of cause and effect. Something which is formed now depends on multiple causes from the past. For example, when someone suddenly scolds or slanders someone else for no apparent reason, people tend to react with self-justification, arguing to their heart's content. But such a reaction cannot bring reconciliation and harmony for both parties, and often only creates more hatred. In such a situation, the better way is for us to just remain calm, and to recognize the feelings in our body and mind. That is enough. When our body and mind actually settle down, we will see the roots of the problem. We see that person had spoken falsely and used unkind words because he or she is suffering. One who is happy will never say anything negative to create suffering in others. Next, we see that a person who uses unkind speech lacks understanding and a clear mind because he or she follows the trail of the ego. Furthermore, we realize how much is actually due to our own weakness, as people may often say some unkind words to us for a few minutes, but we embrace our anger the whole day long. We are swayed by our emotions and dictated to by external circumstances, all from allowing our happiness to depend on each situation, so that when everything goes well, we are happy and things going badly triggers our suffering.

We must realize that sorrow, love, anger, intelligence, and virtue are universal characteristics, not reserved or prioritized for anyone. Why then do not we accept other people's anger as well? We cannot expect others to behave only pleasantly to us when, in fact, sometimes we also have anger towards them. In reality there are always both negative and positive qualities in every individual. People with calm and clear minds know how to treat others with courtesy; people who live with delusion and are not mindful of reality usually experience sadness or happiness depending only on their external circumstances.

To transform suffering into happiness, we must constantly recognize what is happening in our body and mind, and see the present situation in a clear, objective, and honest way. We must not distort and impose upon reality based on our subjective perceptions. We need only to quietly observe the nature of birth and death, and the changing nature of all phenomena, which we see comes and goes just as when we observe a flowing river; in so doing, true peace and happiness will fully come into being within us.

HAPPINESS: A MATTER OF PERSPECTIVE

*Everything in the universe is always changing
and everything is dependent on everything else.
Hidden or manifest, happiness
is a matter of perspective.*

Each individual in this world has a different way of life. Some people have abundant material assets, with fine food and the best clothing, while others are dirt-poor. However, no matter how rich a person is, if he does not have a profound insight into immediate reality, his happiness may be incomplete. Conversely, a person may go through economic hardships, but, with a serene and clear mind, is still able to enjoy the wonders of life. Therefore, happiness or suffering depends upon each individual's perspective.

Who in the world does not long for prosperity and happiness? Clearly, many people pursue this goal, for themselves and their loved ones, and expend all their resources and capabilities working in the hopes of a brighter, more prosperous future. But perhaps this way of thinking is really unsatisfactory, because if we keep searching for happiness in the future, we unwittingly overlook the beauty and the joy of the present moment. For example, family members as well as other positive factors contribute to our happiness, but we do not appreciate and enjoy their presence until they are gone, when it will be too late for regrets. This unfeeling attitude toward our loved ones and obliviousness to current reality can be a great shortcoming and disadvantage for whomever lives without dwelling in the present moment.

Usually, we worry about the next task before even completing the first one. We cannot keep a peaceful mind during dinnertime because we only want to finish the meal soon enough to solve our various problems. With such a busy mind and apprehensive attitude, many people are unable to fully enjoy a happy life.

Certainly, everybody has to work for a living. However, those who have insight into many problems can feel happy while working. This requires each person to look inward and contact his own experiences. And then there is the person who might expect great happiness if he can live with his loved one. However, once his wish comes true, new affliction and suffering will arise. Their dream is fabricated by the self that dwells in delusion, while the truth is quite different. Therefore, happiness depends on each individual's perception, rather than on external circumstances or objective conditions.

A happy individual is, basically, one who has a clear and free mind. His mind is not bound by what happened in the past, nor bothered by expectation of something in the future. If our mind is trapped by these two unreal tendencies, our life will be insecure and miserable.

For this reason, the Buddha taught:

"Do not go after the past,
Nor lose yourself in the future.
For the past no longer exists,

And the future is not yet here.
By looking deeply at things just as they are,
In this moment, here and now,
The seeker lives calmly and freely.
You should be attentive today,
For waiting until tomorrow is too late.
Death can come and take us by surprise"

(MN: Bhaddekaratta Sutra, Page 442)

This sutra affirms happiness is composed of the elements in the present moment. We only need to be fully present to immediate reality, without looking for anything else. On the other hand, human life is very fragile and temporary, nobody can predict how long we will live; therefore, to look for a better future is an erroneous and time-wasting expectation that causes numerous obstacles over the course of a lifetime.

In daily life, we have to look back at ourselves to discover our inheritance. For example, our eyes are a great source of happiness, but we do not pay attention to and treasure them, until dust gets into them or they have injuries.

Some individuals, due to the lack of blessings, are born blind, they cannot see their loved ones nor their surroundings. Their biggest dream is to simply be able to see. Meanwhile, we can see and enjoy everything with our own two eyes – the blue sky, the floating white clouds, the green trees on the roadside, the yellow apricot blossoms, the winding rivers with an abundance of water-hyacinth flowers, and many other beauties of nature; but we ignore such privileges and keep complaining or feeling sorry for ourselves. This is really a waste.

To gain insight into all the problems in life, we need to simply observe our body and mind, and related conditions, in a clear, honest, objective way. In any place and at any time, we should hold that same view when relating with others. Whatever the reality may be, just recognize it as it is, without doing anything else to it. This kind of insight helps keep our mind undisturbed, without striving to attain any particular supreme goal. Indeed, sometimes such effort is only the fabrication of the "wanting self" to satisfy a subtle "self", rather than helping us overcome pain and suffering, and go beyond the cycle of birth and death. The simplest way is, when we walk, we are aware that we are walking; when we sit, we are aware that our entire body is sitting down; when we drink tea, we recognize the good taste of the tea; and nothing else.

This process is quite simple, spontaneous, and does not follow any rules or doctrine. When your mind is not bound to anything, then right in that moment, you are living in freedom and peace. Your perspective toward this world will not reflect any resentment or blame; instead, you will treasure life with appreciation and loving-kindness.

SKILLFUL HANDS

 Our hands are capable of holding all kinds of things, and handling all kinds of duties, such as driving, cooking, dishwashing, cleaning house, using computers, arranging flowers, writing calligraphy, and preparing tea. Any time one part of our body needs something, our hands meet the demand immediately without procrastination or hesitation, discrimination or calculation. Our hands are pleasant and obedient. They accept the direction of the mind regardless of the nature of the job.

Much beauty in the world comes from the accomplishments of hands. High-rise buildings, clean and gleaming asphalt roads, rows of green trees, endless paddy fields with the smell of grain, all of these come from industrious and diligent human hands.

Whenever our body is tired or sore, it is the hands which automatically intervene to soothe the unpleasant feelings. If the body falls, by reflex the hands reach out to protect the body even before the mind has time to react.

Furthermore, our hands know how to take care of each other. If the right hand gets injured, the left hand thoughtfully cares for it, replacing its counterpart in all duties

— and vice versa, if the left hand gets injured. What a marvel it is to have such skillful hands!

Despite their numerous abilities, our hands are impartial and free. Once their work is finished, our hands relax and hold nothing, disengaged and free. It is because our hands ultimately hold nothing that they are able to do many things. If our hands were to permanently hold something in them like a precious object, but not let go of it, then they would not be able to help us eat or drink. The reason the hands have such capability of doing so many different duties is that they let go of everything after the job is done. That is the skillfulness, the wonderful usefulness, and the intelligence of the hands.

In this respect, our mind is worse than our hands even though it leads the whole human body and controls all the senses. If problems arise, the mind cannot solve them with the cleverness of the hands because it has the habits of attachment, of holding firmly on to past experiences. The habits of storing, holding, and entangling the facts of the past, of dreaming, anticipating and impatiently waiting for the future are the roots of many human mental problems. Therefore, when King Du Ton (1706–1729) consulted Zen Master Huong Hai, he was given these verses:

"The swallow hovers in the sky
Its image is reflected in the water.
The swallow has no intention to leave its image in the water.
The water has no desire to preserve the swallow's image."

Through these verses, the Zen master wanted to convey to the King his fundamental idea that we should solve a problem as needed, but, after it is finished, we must let it go, to keep our mind free and at peace. Just like the example of the bird hovering above the lake, neither the bird intends to leave behind any mark, nor does the lake want to retain any bird image. In this way, the lake is able to keep its water clear, calm, and blue, and maintain its peaceful space.

The Zen master's teaching is noticeably clear and concrete. It is simple yet profound because it demonstrates that the ultimate disease of human beings is our clinging to our achievements and our covetousness of pleasant things. We must acknowledge that if our mind is bound by anxiety or lamentation, jealousy or anger, then we will lack happiness and joy. If the mind is not as free as the hands, its knowledge will be narrow and limited, resulting in erroneous, simplistic perceptions of reality. Then one will be truly baffled as to what causes emotional rifts and separation between people. Someone full of pride thinks his viewpoints and knowledge are always correct, which result in self-satisfaction and disregard for other people and their feelings. These rigid thoughts prevent breaking through the everyday deadlock life presents us. The universe always changes and renews, but, due to our simplistic and limited view, we consider it as permanent. Thus, arises the greedy and clinging mind. Due to the habit of the self that distorts and imposes itself upon reality, we are incapable of clearly seeing the true value of our life.

You should look at your hands in their daily activities to recognize their skillfulness, intelligence, and freedom. This will help you look within yourself, quietly listening to each feeling emerging from your mind and simultaneously recognizing the self's habit of fabrication. Once your mind is pure, the clinging self will be abolished, so worries, pettiness, disputes, and grasping will naturally disappear, allowing you to have a new vision of the world. You will see that the sky, plants, flowers, rain, and streams all depend upon each other to develop, yet without being entangled together. The cloud is freely floating, the river calmly flows to the ocean and when favorable conditions are met, rain will come forth to offer cool weather, green plants, and beautiful flowers. All elements of the universe work together in perfect harmony so that each element still keeps its freedom and individuality.

To have joy and happiness in daily life, you must return to yourself to recognize what is happening in your body and mind, and related circumstances, in an objective, clear and honest way. If we live deeply in the present moment, our feelings of anxiety and sorrow from the past, and illusions and expectation about the future, will have no basis for arising. Instead, we will achieve a stable and peaceful mind. Once the mind is clear and pure, the two main factors for happiness will manifest: understanding and loving-kindness. Therefore, we are not deceived into embracing anxiety, fear, sorrow, lamentation, or jealousy, which obliterate our mind and generate suffering and its offshoots. We should let things go, just like our skillful hands that do each job properly, and once finished, release it completely. By doing this in every second of our daily life, stability and happiness are ours to enjoy.

THE BEAUTY OF DAWN

All of us are endowed with opportunities to encounter beauty and spontaneous, romantic feelings. The dawning of these experiences, be they material or emotional, surely impress upon us appreciative memories. Being in love with another person is one of life's most fulfilling experiences.

When our dream of true love becomes a reality, we are more able to embrace beauty, faith, and the joy of being alive. Perhaps that exuberant moment of falling in love is the best foundation for a couple to build long-term happiness. The Vietnamese poet The Lu wrote:

*"The moments we first felt attached to each other
won't be easily forgotten even in a thousand years."*

When looking for someone to marry, men and women seek a good impression based upon a nice outward appearance. A man may love and value a woman's beauty, grace, and charm. And a woman may be attracted to a man who is levelheaded, gentle, and talented, and may want to share the rest of her life with him. Together, they may affirm their true love and commit to a lifelong marriage.

However, the reality of being married is quite different from the initial love experience. Many couples take for granted the beauty of that first "honeymoon phase" and expect it to continue. But what they previously considered the most beautiful thing in the world will not last because they are unable to take care of it and nurture it properly. They are not able to preserve and prolong the beautiful feelings of their wedding day. After the knot is tied and the honeymoon is over, they may become indifferent to each other and no longer value their union. In their family life, they may succumb to a lack of novelty and caring and become bored with each other. Ultimately, each may start looking for more attractive new horizons.

Whether or not the beautiful feeling of being in love can survive for a thousand years as affirmed by the poet, we can all certainly aim for a hundred years of happiness. But the reality is much harder, as all phenomena in this world are always changing. Nothing is constant — so happiness or suffering depends on our attitude right in the present moment. When we love somebody, we tend to attribute to him or her all kinds of virtues, as if he or she is an angel. Later, after we have lived with that person, we realize that everything is not as we expected, and we become disappointed and suffer. But if we know in advance that our lover will someday change, for better or for worse, and if we expect that undesirable things will happen, we will not lament or blame anybody. When we love a person as per our imagination rather than how that person is, despair and affliction will eventually arise.

A broken family is usually the result of a lack of understanding by both parties. Whenever we do not know how to deeply listen to or calmly turn our gaze within, our love will be motivated and directed by sensual instinct rather than by true love. Therefore, building a long-lasting happiness requires that both parties accept each other truthfully and search for mutual understanding and a common direction.

Regarding the foundations for a family's long-term happiness, the Buddha taught:

"If householders, both wife and husband wish to be in one another's lives, so long as this life lasts, and in the future as well, they should have the same faith (saddha), the same moral discipline (silla), the same generosity (dana), the same wisdom (prajna); then they will be in one another's sight as long as this life lasts, and in the future life as well."

(PTS: AN: 4:55,II 61-62).

Strong faith is a basic condition for family happiness and the basis for sustaining the love between couples. Many couples become separated because they do not trust each other. The husband may suspect his wife of having extramarital relations, and someday his wife may also worry about her husband's behavior when he comes home late for no obvious reason. Unfounded suspicions create anxiety and grief for both sides and severely damage the couple's love. Couples must trust each other completely in order to nourish their love and strengthen true marital happiness.

Such a firm faith is established by living according to the social moral standards of one's country. A higher standard consists of taking refuge in the Three Jewels and practicing the Five Precepts, which help open our hearts to the value of life. Another necessary component is the practice of the development of wisdom, whereby our speech, thoughts, and actions become increasingly truthful and beneficial to others. They are the embodiment of the Dharma teachings, illuminating our altruism toward all beings, so that, on contact with this true love, worries and sufferings will cease to exist. With this kind of practice, we demonstrate true love rather than pity. Love without understanding can be harmful to ourselves and others.

According to the Buddha's teachings, we need wisdom in order to behave properly and understand each other. No person, no matter how rich and powerful, who does not vow to transform greed, anger and selfishness, and boredom, will attain understanding and happiness. Those who practice Buddhist wisdom can escape the attachments of greed, anger and delusion, and build true unconditional love. Once our mind becomes calm and clear, we will be more sensitive and flexible, and more capable of behaving appropriately according to each circumstance in daily life. At the same time, we will more easily understand the personal feelings of others, allowing us to have empathy and share in their afflictions and suffering.

In summary, in order to sustain the splendor of love's honeymoon phase, we must put into practice the Buddhist principles of generosity, development of moral discipline, wisdom, and faith. Put more simply, we must constantly observe our body and mind, and deeply understand what is going on in the present moment, resolving problems as needed, and then let go. With such practice, our life will be full of happiness and joy, now and in the future, as if we are always living in the dawning beauty of falling in love.

HAPPINESS IS MUTUAL ACCEPTANCE

Human beings naturally must live, work, and interact with others in society. Interdependence is a necessity for human existence; without it, life would be lonely and dull. To coexist happily with others requires us to understand other people's character and to accept their shortcomings and idiosyncrasies. To live together in harmony, each of us must constantly contemplate and look within ourselves to recognize two different aspects of our being, the wholesome and the unwholesome.

The unwholesome nature in each individual arises from a deluded mind that becomes oblivious of reality. When we are not fully aware of what we are doing, we end up making mistakes in our speech and actions, which, in turn, can cause harm to others and ourselves. Our actions will lack friendliness and kindness, resulting in poor communication between parents and children, husbands and wives, and other family members.

If our mind has not yet awakened and we are not aware of the true nature of its workings, our wholesome nature will not be able to manifest. We then might struggle with loneliness and an inability to share our feelings.

Conversely, if we treat others with an enlightened mind, we will, in turn, be loved, respected, and trusted.

People will come to us to share their life experiences and rely on us for guidance.

Virtuousness is a beautiful, inherent human characteristic. When we quietly observe each activity of our body and mind, the essence of virtue will manifest. The virtuous, honest mind does not seek only to be altruistic but also to be calm and clear in thought, speech, and action. When our mind cannot clearly see the mutual operation of our self and its circumstances, all our actions will be dependent on self, for the sake of self rather than good deeds. A good example is when we do a favor for someone who does not express the kind of gratitude that we would expect: our self-nature will immediately develop anger, hatred, even vengeance. On the other hand, people with clear, virtuous minds are more likely to live their lives with equanimity and joy regardless of how others treat them. As a result, their merit will increase, as well as their longevity. In this way, they will do no harm to anyone and instead be able to contribute their wisdom and experience to others and society. People who are too proud of themselves and too attached to their own knowledge will not be able to learn anything from others; consequently, their social interactions will be defined by narrow-minded behavior.

It is a given that human beings have weaknesses and shortcomings and make mistakes. But they may also possess good characteristics and a virtuous mind. An individual may possess such qualities such as loving-kindness, industriousness, compassion, and tolerance. However, the same person may also have bad habits, inferiority complexes, impatience, envy, and anger. These negative traits create conflict and discord, leading to damaged friendships and broken families. Looking deeply at these two opposite aspects of human behavior, we should acknowledge that as human beings we are exactly so. If we do not accept and tolerate the mistakes of others, how do we expect others to accept our weaknesses and shortcomings? During daily relations with family and friends, we might find occasions for angry or sarcastic expressions. In addition to acrimonious language, we also blame people with our body language and other actions that cause sadness and suffering to our loved ones. Anyone with an impure and disturbed mind can create such unwholesome consequences.

However, the negative aspect of our mentality does not need to be completely eliminated because it helps us to return to ourselves and to look deeply at our mind in order to better understand the nature and harmful effects of anger. From that perspective, we learn precious and practical lessons in order to untangle the impasse between us and others and find a path to freedom and transcendence.

It is not necessary to expect life to be completely pleasant and smooth because obstacles are necessary conditions from which to forge patience and sacrifice, inclusiveness and loving-kindness. Obviously, there is no place in the world without obstacles and negativity unless our mind is totally without greed, anger, and delusion.

To build communication for the sake of mutual family acceptance and happiness, you must first understand yourself. Your thought and your speech must be based on a calm and clear mind; you should not be attached to any rule or convention, prejudicial exclusion, or hatred for anyone. With honest and objective perception, you will attain an explicit assessment of your mind and its far-reaching developments. Through this process, your mind will be free of suffering and your behavior will be positive and wholesome, which will benefit you as well as your community and society.

FLOWERS AND GARBAGE

A flower symbolizes beauty, fragrance, and freshness, so everybody likes to feast their eyes on it and treasure it. Conversely, garbage is dirty and foul smelling. Most people do not pay attention to it and avoid or run as far away from it as possible. Garbage quietly accepts being so badly treated and continues to offer some beautiful gifts to the world.

Trash generates fertilizers that help the gardener grow flowerbeds, vegetables, and fruit trees. Nowadays, farmers try to avoid using chemical fertilizers. Garbage then becomes valuable as an organic fertilizer, that is more nutritious to plants and safer for human health. So do not consider garbage as dirty, bad stuff to be eliminated, but rather as an essential that quietly benefits our life.

The human mind contains these two basic characteristics of flowers and garbage. Our wholesome nature, diligence, kindness, compassion, tolerance, and altruism represent the positive characteristics of our inherent "spiritual flower." When our mind is still and serene, this flower will manifest and offer its fragrant essence. On the other hand, when our mind is subject to greed, anger, sorrow, fear, and jealousy, our spiritual flower garden will produce weeds and garbage. Therefore, a Buddhist practitioner must know how to take care of the "mind's garden," cultivating the flowers and fruits of understanding and loving-kindness in order to offer their fragrance to the world.

The formation of a flower depends on several elements, such as soil, water, air, sunlight, fertilizers and the gardener's labor. The flower and these other elements cannot exist separately: they are interrelated for the flower to manifest. If we only want to look at the upper portion of the flower and cut off its dirty roots, the flower will wither in a few days. Hence, the important role of garbage cannot be ignored in the life of the flower and in human life. This pattern is remarkably similar to our mind, that carries many different kinds of garbage, such as affliction, greed, anger, blame, fear, jealousy, discrimination, and boredom. These negative seeds are hidden in our subconscious, and, when certain conditions are met, they will manifest and dominate our life, leading to insecurity and suffering.

However, if we know how to practice, our "affliction-garbage" will be purified and transformed into "happiness-flowers," offering fragrance to the world. Without the practice of cultivating and watering, these flowers will quickly wither. This principle can be applied in our daily lives to help nurture our happiness. If we do not treasure what we currently have, our happiness will fade away, leaving us in loneliness and sorrow. We must be aware of this truth to avoid personal insecurity and family discord.

Affliction and suffering appear only when our mind is scattered by delusion or dominated by greed or hatred. When we encounter an object, the self immediately reacts, trying to eliminate the object (anger), or coveting it (greed). This reaction habit distorts reality, our subjective perception preventing a right view to manifest. Therefore, we cannot see the importance of garbage to the formation of the flower; in the same way, suffering helps us understand the true nature of human life.

If we do not learn this valuable lesson about our suffering, we will lack the ability to transform suffering into happiness for ourselves and rescue others from difficult and complicated situations. A good example is if we hear there is a precious pearl hidden in a trashcan: are we willing to pull the pearl out of the filthy trash? So, being either overly-hasty in reaction or being in the habit of denial are basic causes of suffering.

All human beings, without exception, from the rich and powerful to the poor and underprivileged, must go through difficulties and, from time to time, face affliction and suffering. However, if you know how to cultivate a pure and calm mind, you will not be trapped in unwholesome situations.

When your pure mind recognizes a false perception or judgment, originating from a sense of a self, born of greed, anger, or ignorance, you will be free to enjoy the beauty of the rivers, mountains, trees and flowers, without being attached to any thought of grasping or rejecting.

All phenomena and conditions in this universe always change and begin anew. You cannot hang on and expect your possessions to last forever. You need to get in touch with reality, as it is, in the here and now. Do not try to impose your opinion or past prejudice on current reality; instead, you must try to find your own appropriate solution to problems without copying any stereotype created by others. If you apply this principle constantly in your daily activities, you will be able to create good relations, and will do no harm to other beings, be they as small as a worm or an ant. Your view will be truthful and fresh in all domains of social life.

To see the non-dual nature of flower-garbage, suffering-happiness, and affliction-Bodhi, (suffering-awakening), you must look within yourself and take care of your "spiritual flower," enhancing its beauty and fragrance. That is, when your mind wanders off, return to being fully present to reality, such as it is.

Once your body-mind and its circumstance are illuminated, you will clearly see the essential interdependence between yourself and the world, flowers and garbage. Thus, you will no longer hate, avoid, or exclude anything if you know how to transform garbage into flowers, dissatisfaction and suffering into joy and happiness.

BREATHING: A BODY-MIND THERAPY

Occasionally in our daily lives, we encounter extreme stress, discomfort, and insecurity. These emotions are affected by many external factors, but they arise mainly from our mind. If we still have greed, anger and delusion, we will be dominated and bound by affliction and suffering. The Buddhist method of mindful breathing, to heal and transform these three poisons, is a miraculous therapy eradicating these roots of human suffering. The breath is like a mother nurturing us to grow up. It functions continuously, constantly, day and night, non-stop. Whether we are awake or asleep, breathing diligently moves air into our bloodstream, nourishing all the cells of our body. If breathing stops, after a few minutes all bodily functions and activities will cease, along with all the power and the glory we spent years building up. Human life is as fragile and temporary as the morning dew, a flash of lightning.

"One day, Buddha asked the Sangha how long human life lasts, the first Bhikkhu says in a few days, the second says about the time of eating a meal and the last one says human life only last in one breath. Buddha praised the last Bhikkhu of his Dharma understanding." (The Sutra of Forty-Two Chapters)

Daily practice of mindful breathing, in and out, improves blood circulation and prevents many diseases. In yoga and meditation centers, attendees learn how mindful breathing brings physical refreshment and mental tranquility. With such practice, breath grows longer and deeper, resulting in more flowing into oxygen flowing into the body, and more toxic elements being flushed out. Cell metabolism is vitalized. A serene mind follows meditation sessions, and sometimes a strong appetite, as well.

Nowadays, more and more people in the West are familiar with meditation. They spend more time in meditation practice as it helps transform daily life's conflicts and insecurities into a free and peaceful way of living. But even while living in abundant material comfort, many Westerners are still unable to release their mental confusion and difficulties.

Meanwhile, scientists have begun to do more research in meditation. Dr. Do Hong Ngoc, medical doctor and author, has written extensively on the therapeutic effects of meditation. From his experience treating his own illness, he has obtained new findings about the human body and new approaches for treatment of illness. He affirms:

"From a medical doctor's perspective, I pay attention to a simple but effective meditation method which is not mysterious, sublime or difficult; a kind of daily meditation which has been carefully investigated and widely applied in health care facilities. It brings unexpected effects in the treatment of stress-related diseases such as anxiety and other illnesses', which are caused by individual ways of life and which have no response from usual therapy by medications."

(Do Hong Ngoc: Breathing and Meditation).

In terms of mental illness, awareness of breathing has been proven to be effective in calming feelings of despair, anxiety, fear and insecurity. Regardless of wealth, fame, or social rank, obstacles and hardships are quite common in this world. Sometimes, we might encounter unwanted situations prompting unbearable affliction and suffering. The best way to overcome such hardship is to return to our breath, to our true self, and to listen deeply and recognize these emotions. In that way, we can clearly see the dynamics of how of greed, anger, and delusion work.

Suffering is always caused by the ego, leading to our false views. We live in delusion and in denial, shut off from reality. Our attachment to our ego-self will generate unwholesome feelings; freedom will be lost; suffering will arise, along with an intention to grasp after the good and reject the bad. Returning to conscious breathing is the basic initial method for transforming affliction and suffering into joy and happiness. Regarding this practice, the Buddha taught:

"The Bhikkhu finds a forest, or a foot of a big tree, or an empty house, he sits in the cross-legged position, with straight body, he maintains his presence in the here and now through mindfulness. Breathing in, he knows with his clear mind that he is breathing in. Breathing out, he knows with his clear mind that he is breathing out. Having a long breathing in, he is aware that he has a long breathing in. Having a short breathing out, he is aware that he has a short breathing out."

(Plum Village Chanting and Recitation Book).

In many meditation centers, practitioners use the mind to direct the breathing. This kind of practice benefits the beginner's health. However, to attain real peace and liberation, we must let go of the idea of manipulating the breath, as taught by Buddha: "When the in-breath is short, you take note of the fact that it is short, and when the in-breath is long, you take note of the fact that it is long." We should follow the breath as it is and not interfere with it: we merely quietly observe the coming and going of a breath, feeling it as it is, not using the mind to control it. By maintaining our presence in the here and now, along with recognizing our breath, we can realize the correct method of mindfulness, and with a pure and clear mind, we can escape all afflictions. Nothing else can dominate and influence our life.

In summary, breath is particularly important in our life. If we know how to return to ourselves and take good care of our breath, we will be able to discover so much beauty in the world and recognize the therapeutic potential of our breath for transforming the energy of grief and suffering into the energy of joy and happiness for ourselves and for others.

HAPPINESS IS MANIFEST

It was a Sunday morning with warm weather and a clear blue sky over the beautiful and peaceful landscape. After days of hustle and bustle in the crowded cities, many tourists came to find some relaxation in this mountainous region. A man in his forties sat on a rock on the edge of a lakeshore and sipped tea while quietly staring at his fishing rod. Suddenly, a tourist came and sat beside him and began talking to him:

"You are still young why don't you look for a job? If you continue fishing, how long till you have enough fish to afford you a wealthier life?"

The fisherman asked the tourist, "What kind of job do you think will bring me a prosperous and happy life?"

The tourist replied, "Well, you could be a laborer."

"How come I will be better off with the meager salary of a laborer?"

The tourist added, "You can start as worker, then after being evaluated by the manager, you can ask for a different position with a higher salary such as secretary or something else."

"As far as I know working as a secretary, far from getting rich, one just has enough to survive," the fisherman answered.

The tourist replied, "As a secretary, you will have the opportunity to meet a lot of people, and you can borrow money to build up your own business. And who knows, you may become a director of a thriving company."

The fisherman said, "If I become a director then so what?"

"As a director, you can ask your employees to work for you, so you have more time to build your own house, buy whatever you want, and travel with your family. You can visit different resorts where you can drink tea while enjoying the clean air and peaceful scenery."

The fisherman said, "Oh, don't you see that I am drinking tea and contemplating the beauty of nature right now? I do not need to be a director to enjoy the beautiful landscape of this mountainous area. Besides, as a director, how can I have enough time to fully appreciate the beauty of nature just as it is at in this present moment?"

After this short conversation, the tourist became aware of how little he really knew about the true value of life. Before, he thought happiness would come when one had a stable career and sufficient material comfort. Now he realized how superficial this kind of thinking is. Wealthy, powerful people of high social rank still suffer. The world news reports such daily, tragic events as murder due to power struggles, suicides after broken love, or lives lost in war or natural disasters: these unfortunate events show that people may encounter more suffering than happiness. It was a good opportunity for him to visit this resort and discuss with an ordinary fisherman about simple joys that people usually overlook.

From this story, we learn that we tend to look for happiness in the future. We expect happiness whenever we attain a goal. A student expects happiness after graduation; once graduated, he thinks that a good job will bring him happiness. After having a stable career, he still longs to owning a house and have a good family in order to be happy. Then he has to spend all his time and energy to earn money to take care of his family and think of some other projects. And so, it goes. People always look forward, wait, anticipate, and hope for happiness in the future. Meanwhile, when we say to newlyweds "Wishing you a hundred years of happiness" we also mean "We wish you to be happy every moment, every day, every month without waiting for the one hundredth year."

Of course, when we solve a problem or achieve a project, we feel satisfied and happy. However, waiting until a job is finished is of no benefit; why don't we find peace and joy while working rather than waiting until the job is done? Besides, in human society, jobs never end.

Chapter Four of the Lotus Sutra, on faith, tells of the idiocy of a beggar. He was the son of a wealthy man but was a wanderer, not wanting to return home to receive his inheritance as his father expected. With compassion and wisdom, the father used skillful means to help him get out of poverty and finally come home to enjoy a prosperous and happy life. We all do have that idiocy. We possess a treasure in the present moment, but we ignore and abandon it. Instead, we keep running after some unreal, future happiness. Of course, everyone should have plans how to use our energy to make life better for our family and society. However, in any circumstance, we must always look within ourselves to find the true value of life.

Happiness will manifest once you dwell in the present moment and listen deeply to your body and mind. This method helps you get a better view of all phenomena such as rivers, green trees, flowers, clouds, and the blue sky. Anything you get in touch with, even a bad person, will become a valuable lesson for you.

You would do well to set aside some time every day to sit still and listen deeply to the needs of your body and mind, that require rest and balance after a busy and stressful day. You must let your body and mind return to their basic nature by practicing total relaxation, recognizing the in-breath and out-breath as well as the feelings arising from your body, in a state of stillness and clarity. Through this practice, your body and mind will be at ease; meanwhile, negative emotions of the day will disappear by themselves. If you can focus your body and mind every day with diligence, no matter where you are, then, whatever difficult situation you may encounter, you are master of your mind and able to fully enjoy peace and happiness.

MOTHER'S ADVICE

"You must put some thought and attention into everything you do, my dear."

This is a common expression used by a Vietnamese mother to teach her children, mostly her daughters. It is not limited to any region but widespread throughout Vietnam. As a result, the daughter eventually becomes more careful and more attentive to what she is doing.

"Có ý" in Vietnamese means we must put our thought, our mind in anything that we get in touch with. "Có tứ" means we must observe what is happening in a clear, correct, and truthful manner. For this purpose, our body and mind must co-exist in the present moment, to help us clearly see the current situation, and maintain a still mind when facing any conflict or obstacle in life.

While doing chores around the house, we can train ourselves to carefully observe all our body movements, from the stretching of our limbs to the feeling of the cold floor under our feet. We must also recognize our breathing in and breathing out while listening deeply to surrounding sounds. If we can focus our mind that way, our job will be more fruitful. Driving our car is another example of bringing benefits to us and to others, if we know how to focus our mind only on driving, instead of hurrying to reach home or the workplace. Without proper attention, we may run the red light, causing a traffic jam or even a serious accident. So, a simple trip could become a miserable journey full of pain, affliction and insecurity. In fact, stopping at the red light would be a good opportunity to look within ourselves, relax our body-mind, and let go of any anxiety or sorrow. With a calm mind, our trip will be much more enjoyable, and we can have peace and happiness while driving without waiting to reach our destination. Although it is somewhat old fashioned, the mother's advice is highly effective in solving daily problems. This can be considered a miraculous mantra to help people live in peace and happiness in the present moment. It is also like the practice of mindfulness, a core method of mental mastery taught in the Satipatthana Sutra (The Four Foundations of Mindfulness).

Perhaps thanks to the widespread Buddhist practice during the Lý and Trần Dynasties, the Vietnamese people have been familiar with Zen meditation. With its transmission from generation to generation, common people have changed the sophisticated word "mindfulness" into a simple but important expression "có ý, có tứ" in the mother's teaching. The Vietnamese ancestors obviously have left a valuable cultural treasure, so that their descendants will find true happiness by practicing the mindful way in all aspects of their life.

Living in awareness and mindfulness is certainly a noble and peaceful way of life for whomever longs for moral and spiritual development. However, due to a life of busily running after material comfort, many of us end up forgetting our inherent pure mind. Mindfulness is knowing how to focus on what we are doing. Awareness allows us to passively observe when we walk that we are walking. This practice may be applied in all activities of daily living such as eating and drinking. Usually, we are in a state of anticipation, waiting for a happy future, and so forget the present moment. As such, we lose our freedom to see the true nature of life which always exists in the here and now. The blue sky, the white clouds, the green trees along the road, the fragrant flowers are wonders nature offers us, but we think we do not have time to enjoy them. Our parents and all the dear ones around us are also factors contributing to our happiness, but we do not appreciate their valuable presence, disregarding their love or sometimes totally ignoring them. Until one day, when our loved ones pass away, leaving us with regrets and sorrow.

Living "thoughtfully and carefully" (có ý, có tứ) is the basic condition for nurturing our inherent compassion and understanding. However, if we are living in delusion or ignoring reality, loving-kindness and understanding may not have the opportunity to develop. In applying this simple mother's advice, "just put some thought and attention into everything you do, my dear," we can transform affliction and sorrow into joy and happiness not only for us but also for our family and our community.

GRATITUDE

Gratitude is one of our most highly valued, cultivated, and respected virtues. It is also necessary to attain true happiness. When one has gratitude toward all sentient beings, one will cherish and respect life. One will have no intention to eliminate or destroy what one dislikes; on the contrary, one is more capable of accepting and loving what he or she dislikes. Therefore, his or her happiness will naturally manifest.

Buddhism teaches us that there are four kinds of great favors bestowed upon us: from our parents, our teachers, our society and country, and from all sentient beings. Such a division into four kinds of favors is only arbitrary; it helps clarify to whom we have to be grateful. However, with wisdom and compassion, a Buddhist practitioner will return favors without any preference. Such gratitude should not be only expressed in words of praise, but also through real, concrete actions. People must know how to transform affliction and suffering by cultivating a clear and peaceful mind. Such a mind is not so busy striving for position and privilege. Fame and power naturally come to them due to the dynamics of the law of cause-condition-effect, without any negative intention fabricated by the self (ego).

A clear and peaceful mind is needed to recognize gratitude as it helps one to understand the mutual relations and interdependence of all sentient and non-sentient beings in the universe. Everyone depends on each other to exist, and vice versa. Human life is the product of a combination of factors, including such physical conditions as our parents' genes, sunlight, air from the atmosphere, food processing methods, and such mental factors as our training from our family, school, and society. Our well-being also depends on the wisdom and virtue of our national leaders, who help avoid foreign invasion or civil wars. Similarly, we owe gratitude to nature. We cannot survive if the atmosphere and the environment are polluted. With such a comprehensive understanding of the interdependence of all creatures on earth, we will be able to realize that one individual's bad actions may cause a chain of bad effects to all of society. The false view that one's existence is independent of others results in a covetous mind, which, in turn, leads to dispute, enmity, afflictions, and suffering.

On a larger scale, we are aware that nowadays many human development projects create imbalance in the ecological environment, leading to natural disasters: storms and floods, due to deforestation; air and water pollution due to industrial wastes; global warming, due to the burning of oil, coal and gas; and so on. Human beings are beginning to realize that these selfish actions on any scale not only creates individual suffering but also damages the quality of life in the whole world.

Therefore, gratitude does not simply mean words or gifts, but should be expressed thru sincere thoughts and concrete actions. Keeping a clear, peaceful mind and the goal of bringing happiness to others is a correct practice of gratitude. Acknowledging the multiple factors contributing to our daily meals, or the multiple conditions leading to our success and happiness is another way to express our gratitude. Doing charity work to help the underprivileged and the poor is another obvious way to show our gratitude. To appreciate Mother Earth's favors, we should only consume products according to our basic needs and should not do anything that unnecessarily contributes to the destruction of our healthy environment.

Finally, a subtle way to manifest our gratitude is to be mindful of the consequences of our actions. Keep in mind that the simple and peaceful way of life of each individual can contribute greatly to the peace and prosperity of the whole world. By building a strong foundation of gratitude, we will be able to guide future generations in properly paying their debts to parents, teachers, our nation, and all sentient beings.

SPRING IS HERE

After a cold, barren winter, people welcome the warm, bright, spring season with its new buddings and blossoming flowers, as a signal of joy and a promising future ahead. Human beings and all things in the universe change, following the periodic cycle of four seasons, each having its own way to contribute to the creation of life. However, it is likely that almost everyone is longing for the spring season, as a symbol of beauty, hope, and vitality. Thus, if anyone appears gloomy and sad, people may say, "There is no spring in his face." Anyone with a fearful, anxious, insecure mind will never be able to appreciate the marvelous beauty of spring. On the contrary, people with a clear, peaceful and joyful mind are able to live in a long-lasting spring. A famous Vietnamese poet wrote:

"What landscape wouldn't be tinged by your own gloom?
Yet when you feel down, can what you see bring you joy?"
(The Tale of Kieu; Nguyen Du)

Nature is always thus. Flowers blossom and wither, in accordance with the dynamics of how the universe operates: formation, stability, disintegration, and void. Looking into this natural cycle of change, we see we can have joy or sorrow depending on our attitude in that moment. To attain a happy life, we would do well to follow this teaching of the Buddha:

"Bhikkhus, possessing five other qualities, a bhikkhu dwells happily in this very life—without distress, anguish, and fever—and with

the breakup of the body, after death, a good destination can be expected for him. What five? Here, a bhikkhu is endowed with faith, has a sense of moral shame, has moral dread, and is energetic and wise. Possessing these five qualities, a bhikkhu dwells happily in this very life—without distress, anguish, and fever—and with the breakup of the body, after death, a good destination can be expected for him."

PTS: AN 5.3: Suffering (Dukkha Sutta)

English translations by Bhikkhu Bodhi, 2012

If we are determined to study the Dharma, we must have faith in the noble disciples, in the karmic law of cause and effect, and take refuge in the Three Jewels. If we have shame when making mistakes, know how to properly repent, always live with mindfulness and awareness, and diligently accomplish good deeds, in order to transform suffering and attain perfect wisdom, we then can enjoy freedom and happiness, right in this present life; and, after death, we will be reborn in a peaceful realm.

Human beings eventually make mistakes, but if we know how to properly repent, and refresh our mind, we may have transcendental experiences in life. Spring does not only come at the beginning of each year; instead, the true spring will manifest whenever our mind is in a state of stillness and clarity.

Many people are subject to anxiety during the Lunar New Year, with so many negative feelings in their hearts that they become totally insensitive to what is happening around them. They are unable to enjoy the fragrance of the spring season due to such difficulties as family troubles and economic hardships. But is enjoyment of spring a privilege for rich people only? It is not, because underprivileged or poor people can welcome a joyful and warm new year, depending on how they behave with each other in the family and in society. If they know how to maintain a close relationship with good people, learn from the wise, sustain love and harmony among family members, and accept reality as such, as it is in the present moment, they certainly will enjoy a happy life. They will have apricot flowers blossoming all year 'round in their heart. This free spirit is beautifully expressed in Zen master Man Giac's famous verses:

*"Don't say all flowers are gone now that Spring is nearing its end.
An apricot branch in the front yard has just blossomed overnight."*

An immortal apricot flower will manifest only when the mind is tranquil and clear. If we do not know how to return to ourselves, contemplating reality and our circumstances, then images and sounds will easily entrap us. We see only changes in the external conditions of a phenomenon, but not in their true nature, since spring and flowers are still present. Ordinarily, all things in the universe assume form and then decompose; but with deep insight, the Zen master's view is beyond all concepts of birth and death, of being and non-being. Therefore, at any time and in any circumstance, he is always free and peaceful with an apricot flower ever blooming in his heart.

In Vietnamese Buddhism, spring is joyfully called Maitreya spring. People attend ceremonies at the temple, pray for themselves and others to enjoy a new year of prosperity and peace. Spring offers an opportunity for Buddhists to get in touch with and learn the vows of Maitreya Buddha, the symbol of equanimity and selflessness. Letting go of what is difficult is one of his great virtues. Facing lies and slander from others, he remains relaxed and undisturbed. The five children seen surrounding him symbolize five desires: the temptations of beauty, fame, fine perfume, delicious taste, and sensual pleasure, which tend to dominate and control the mind. Maitreya Buddha remains indifferent when facing these temptations. Without awareness and mindfulness, people will be dominated by greed, anger, and delusion; meanwhile, with wisdom and compassion, the enlightened Bodhisattvas always freely mingle with us in daily life in order to rescue sentient beings from suffering. Therefore, on one hand, spring offers our heart fresh apricot flowers, and, on the other hand, spring gives us an opportunity to better see the noble path leading to joy and peace. That is the true meaning of the celebrating the spring of Maitreya Buddha.

To maintain an everlasting spring season, Buddhist disciples must always look within themselves, keep their mind calm, live life as it is, and avoid being controlled by circumstances. This is the best way to enjoy the beauty of nature, as well as the splendor of an everlasting spring.

THE ART OF TEA DRINKING

In Asian society, from common people to intellectuals, everyone knows how to drink tea. Yet it requires a special art, in order to establish communication between members of a family and other groups, enhancing understanding and love.

We sit together drinking tea and talk about business, we discuss and evaluate the daily news, and so forth, but we are not truly there to enjoy the taste of the tea nor are we fully in touch with the friends with whom we are sitting with. Obviously, drinking tea in such an impatient, hasty way wastes time. Also, the habit of discussion and argument over a cup of tea results in conflict and discord. Novices in the temples are cautioned "While on the plank bed, you must not huddle over the tea, sit up late into the night, or engage in silly talk." Instead, it would be better to drink tea to calm one's mind, enrich one's knowledge, and open one's heart to love and compassion. To reach such a goal, we must contemplate and treat drinking tea as an art.

Art is defined as "the expression or application of human creative skill and imagination related to one's production in any profession." A clever soccer player must have his own personal art of soccer as well as his skill. Tea drinking needs to be a special art, for people to fully enjoy its taste. This requires, in part, a mind at ease and peace. If you really focus your mind on the teacup and avoid distractions, then in that present moment you may recognize the art of tea drinking.

In China, Korea, and Japan people have their own interesting way of tea drinking. Many Japanese people are familiar with traditional practices and special techniques of making and sharing tea with a refined art and attitude. They call it the tea ceremony, or the Way of Tea.

In Vietnam, although there is not yet a Way of Tea, almost everybody enjoys a few cups of tea in the morning, before going out to the farm or driving to work. Tea is also a necessity for poets, writers, and artists because it helps them to stay alert with a clear mind.

In monasteries, a monk's temple lifestyle is quite simple. Ordained monastics consider tea as their friend. A few cups of tea are enough for a gathering. While enjoying tea, monks often share their recent religious practices and experiences following the Buddha's Path. Often, the negative emotions from misunderstanding or conflict that naturally occurs among brothers, or between teachers and disciples, are easier to be quickly resolved by getting together at tea ceremonies. This is a unique method of building bonds of brotherhood. It requires everyone to practice and follow the Way of Tea.

Inspired by the Way of Tea, I would like to express my feelings with this poem:

"Each cup of tea is sipped
with leisure and a boundless empty mind.
A cup of tea at early dawn,
and the mind's garden is filled with flowers and fragrance."
(Thich Vien Ngo)

When lifting your teacup, you should be aware of what is happening in your body and mind and the present situation. In other words, you should fully get in touch with the reality of the here and now, without letting your mind aimlessly wander. With this approach, you will be able to enjoy the taste of the tea, hence peace and happiness. That is the Way of Tea's peak of mindfulness.

Due to pressures from school or work, people rarely have free time to enjoy even a sip of tea. While toiling night and day to make money, people hastily seek more and more material comforts. Therefore, family members rarely have occasion to be together for communication and sharing feelings with each other. Even if the quality of their material life improves, insecurity and impasses in their spiritual life still occur, due to the lack of communication and understanding between parents and children, husbands and wives, or among friends and co-workers. To resolve such problems, it is good to make time for being in a quiet, tranquil environment, to achieve a total relaxation of body and mind, passively observing what is happening. Along with this kind of practice, a cup of tea leads to a peaceful and clear mind.

The art of tea is quite simple, not too formal, yet adding to our quality of life. It is better to forgo a great deal of formality and ritual. Instead, from the time of tea preparation to the moment you raise the cup and drink the tea, you center your mind on the tea and are fully present in the moment without mind wandering. That is the profound meaning of the Way of Tea.

LISTENING DEEPLY TO PROMOTE HAPPINESS

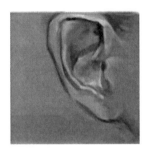

Each member in a family or community always has opportunities to learn from others. However, living together in a group, people do encounter moments of disappointment and discord. If human beings are dominated or fettered by greed, anger, and delusion, afflictions and suffering will always still exist. Therefore, we ought to share our experiences, while listening deeply to other people's attitudes and aspirations. This is the most effective way to understand and love others.

The Exalted One taught:

"One thing, monks, when it comes to pass in the world, do so to the profit, to the happiness of many folks, come to pass the welfare, the profit, to the happiness of devas and mankind. What one thing? Concord in the Order (Sangha). Indeed, monks, when the Order is harmonious, there are not mutual quarrels, mutual abuse, mutual exclusiveness and mutual betrayals. Thereupon those who are at variance are reconciled, and between those who are at one, there is further growth of unity" (PTS: ITHIVUTTAKA: As it was said: The Ones: I: IX, 123)

According to Buddhist tradition, every half month, all monks in the temple sit together to exchange and share their experiences of practice; each has to talk about his own shortcomings and mistakes in the past half month, so the Sangha can shine the light and educate him. If he is determined to practice repentance along with the guidance and feedback from his brothers in the Sangha, it will be easier for him to transform his disturbed mind into a calm and clear one. Then he must read the precepts to remind himself and other Bhikkhus about cultivating moral disciplines. This ritual is called Uposatha practice or cleansing the mind. Thanks to this method of holding discussions to maintain harmony in the monastic community, the Bhikkhus can attain peace of mind and a better knowledge of ethics.

Thus, once entering monastic life, every monk or nun not only needs diligent daily practice to transform greed, anger, and delusion, but also needs to regularly participate, every half month, in the Sangha meeting for mental purification practice, in order to clearly see and reduce his or her shortcomings, as much as possible. Meanwhile, Buddhist laypersons, who are busy working for a living and participating in other activities, will face afflictions and insecurity. No matter how busy they are, it is good to gather a few times a month for the same purpose of untying daily gridlock and looking for better ways to reduce suffering.

The above-mentioned sutra affirms that harmony in the Sangha is the foundation of individual happiness, which can spread to the community. This helps develop wholesome behavior and enhances the strength of the Sangha. If masters and disciples in a monastery, even during simple teatime, establish good communication and share their negative personal shortcomings, and contribute positive opinions regarding the Sangha's activities – they not only provide a happy and peaceful environment for themselves but also help followers and the community to maintain a way of life free from affliction and suffering. Therefore, in monasteries, where monks or nuns live together in the spirit of the Six Harmonies, equally sharing benefits and responsibilities without discrimination, their Sangha will be able to flourish and prosper.

These are the Six Harmonies according to The Exalted One:

Harmony in living together (all bedrooms are the same for everybody)
Harmony in speaking without conflicts (speaking without quarrels)
Harmony in consideration and approval of viewpoints (all opinions should be respected)
Harmony in observing the same precepts (Precepts should be observed by all)
Harmony in solving all views (views are explained and shared)
Harmony in sharing benefits (equality in sharing the requisites)

These harmonies, on one hand, prevent unwholesome phenomena from arising, and, on the other hand, help people live together joyfully and peacefully. That is why the Buddha firmly insists that the harmony of the Sangha be applied by humanity in the pursuit of happiness.

When people live in their community with the spirit of trust and harmony, faith and strength will develop, leading to success and accomplishment in all domains of social life. However, complete harmony in human relations requires that each person develop a capacity for deep listening and contemplation in all circumstances, hence, understanding and loving- kindness within the community.

In a context of family life, if there is no opportunity for husband and wife, parents and children to listen and share their personal attitudes, communication will be impossible, creating a dark atmosphere. All family members will fail to accept each other and to live in happiness. The same situation applies to a company where the leaders do not listen to the staff's opinions, nor organize meetings to resolve gridlock and achieve agreement, in order to grow. So, the practice of deep listening is a cornerstone for a company's success.

Along with social development, the material standard of life becomes higher, but there is not necessarily a parallel improvement in communication, between family members, teachers and students. Negativity in the family and society can manifest in more separation and divorce, fewer children who care for their parents, more disputes over family inheritance, more lawsuits, more at-risk youth becoming involved in robbery, gambling, and drug addiction, all leading to deeper social insecurity.

Deep contemplation will help us realize that these complicated issues originate from lack of empathy and understanding. It may take only a bit of time for tea, in a quiet corner with some fresh flowers, where people can sit together and clearly express their feelings – and then most of their problems will be solved easily. When our mind is pure, our words will be kinder, loving-kindness and equanimity will be greater, and those who listen will warmly appreciate our presence.

To promote happiness, each person must be aware of his or her speech, thoughts, and actions by regularly practicing introspection to identify emerging feelings. Such contemplation helps reveal our innately pure mind. With that insight, deep listening to someone's needs is a simple way we can all practice for the sake of our own happiness as well as for the well-being of society.

SELF-TRANSFORMATION TO FULFILL FILIAL PIETY

Filial piety is a fundamental standard of morality. Caring for our parents is a natural responsibility. We should never wonder why or set conditions upon it. Our debt to our parents is incalculably immense. For this reason, the World Honored One said,

"Monks, I declare that there are two persons one can never repay. What two? One's mother and father. Even if one should carry about one's mother on one shoulder and one's father on the other, and while doing so should live a hundred years, reach the age of one hundred years, and if one should attend to them by anointing them with balms, by massaging, bathing, and rubbing their limbs, and they should even void their excrement there – even by that would one not do enough for one's parents, nor would one repay them. Even if one were to establish one's parents as the supreme lords and rulers over this earth so rich in the seven treasures, one would not do enough for them, nor would one repay them. For what reason? Parents are of great help to their children, they bring them up, feed them and show them the world." (PTS: AN 2: iv,2; I 62-62)

We come into this world through our parents' love. After months of pregnancy followed by painful delivery then years of bringing up their children, our parent's task is quite difficult and strenuous. The love for their children is unconditional. They are satisfied only when their children are healthy and well-behaved. In Vietnamese tradition, these aids are considered "as high as a mountain, as deep as the ocean. Even if it takes a lifetime for children to care for their parents, it is still never long enough to return their favors. This is well-explained in the Buddha's teachings.

If a child diligently takes good care of his parents, he or she will be considered a filial child. This care should be expressed daily in concrete and honest ways by his speech, thoughts and actions. To be successful and complete, filial duty must be based on a pure and clear mind.

In fact, the greatest gift a child can offer is his or her lifestyle, reflecting good health, ethical conduct, and harmonious behavior toward others. On the contrary, if children lack basic virtues and a good cultural background, fail to protect and help each other, and do not care about brotherhood, then no matter how many material gifts and how much physical comfort they are provided, they are not considered filial children. Therefore, filial piety refers to a process of learning and contemplating our actions, speech and thoughts in order to comply with human standards of morality.

In the Sigalaka Sutra, the Buddha taught:

"There are five ways in which a son should minister to his mother and father. He should think having been supported by them, I will support them. I will perform their duty for them. I will keep up the family tradition. I will be worthy of my heritage. After my parents' deaths, I will distribute gifts on their behalf. And, homeowner, there are five ways in which the parents, so ministered to by their son, will reciprocate: they will restrain from evil, support him in doing good, teach him some skill, find him a suitable wife, and, in due time, hand over his inheritance to him." (Worshipping the Six Directions: (DN 31: Sigalaka Sutra; III)

The five ways for the children and the five ways for the parents will help the family to be free from fear and to live in peace.

In addition to the children's duty toward parents, for the sake of family happiness, parents must also fulfill responsibilities toward their children.

However, there are parents who do not fulfill their duties, possibly due to their bad karma. They do not set virtuous examples for children, and, instead, are a bad influence on them. In this case, the Buddha taught:

"Here, monks, one who encourages his unbelieving parents, settles and establishes them in faith; who encourages his immoral parents, settles and establishes them in moral discipline; who encourages his stingy parents, settles and establishes them in generosity; who encourages his ignorant parents, settles and establishes them in wisdom — such a one, monks, does enough for his parents: he repays them and more than repays them for what they have done." (AN 2: iv, 2; I 62-62)

In Buddhism, each human existence is determined by karma. Some crave for status and privilege, others for money and beauty. However, karma can be transformed according to each person's level of spiritual practice. Therefore, the most practical way for children to return their parents' favor is to create conditions and motivations for them to take refuge in the Three Jewels, help them to transform the bad karma in order to attain a happy and peaceful life. Setting an example for parents in the cultivation of moral values and accomplishing good deeds will bring benefits not only in this life but in many future lives. Furthermore, children also get blessings once their parents live well in their life and in their faith following the religious path.

Unfortunately, many things do not happen according to one's expectations. Despite their love and respect toward parents, due to difficult economic situations, children may not have time to care for their parents. Facing great hardship, people often promise to repay their parents' debts some day in the future. Regrettably, since life is subject to impermanence, our parents may pass away before we could fulfill our filial piety.

Anyone lucky enough to still have both parents should cherish their presence. You ought to spend more time talking to and listening to them, and to understand their daily needs in old age. Let them enjoy their time as grandparents, but do not ask them to take care of your children.

In Buddhism, it takes a great deal of insight to fully enjoy parents' love and to fulfill filial piety. You should return to yourself, to see whether your thoughts and actions truly reflect your filial duty. If your mind is in delusion, your behavior toward your loved ones may include selfishness and calculation, which originate from the self-based in greed, anger, and ignorance rather than from true love and compassion. Only when your mind is pure and calm you will know how and when to transform your speech, thoughts, and actions in order to satisfy your parents' needs. This is the essential Buddhist teaching concerning filial piety toward one's parents and ancestors.

INTROSPECTION GENERATES COMPASSION

Love is indispensable for true happiness. Without it, life would be meaningless. However, we rarely turn inward to see and understand the true value of life and to love ourselves and others. When our body and mind come into a state of unity, inherent wisdom will manifest, helping love to emerge. Wisdom is the key opening the door to joy and true happiness.

In the Tran dynasty, scholar Tue Trung was a layman who practiced the Buddha's teachings and attained enlightenment. King Tran Thanh Tong entrusted Tue Trung with guiding prince Tran Kham in learning and practicing meditation, in search of ripening wisdom along the Path of the Buddha. Before returning to the Royal Court, the prince asked Master Tue Trung:

"What is the core of Zen?"
"Illuminating yourself is your task, and it cannot be done by others," replied *Tue Trung.*
(The Analects of Tue Trung Thuong Si).

The answer is short, but it contains the essence of Zen. It implies that the core of joy and happiness is inherent in each of us and cannot be found elsewhere. We only need to carefully and thoroughly exercise introspection to see the multiple conditions present contributing to happiness. King Tran Nhan Tong, the former prince Tran Kham, who, thanks to his deep understanding of the Dharma, later became the

First Patriarch of the **Trúc Lâm Yên Tử** Zen tradition.

Turning inward means looking within ourselves and our current reality; in other words, returning to the here and now in order to fully appreciate whatever is manifesting. Looking within helps us see the dynamics of our body-mind and current circumstances. Looking back is having a sense of awareness where the mind is not deluded or distracted by its environment. As such, one will recognize what is arising in one's mind, and, in turn, not allow it to be dominated or controlled by one's ego.

We tend to forget this process of looking back at ourselves. A good example is when we are in a shopping mall, where we are mostly controlled by external circumstances and our habits of buying. The same situation can also be applied in other activities where we are directed by a pattern of self to follow a certain stereotype. A few offensive words may trigger the self to immediately react by analyzing and judging in terms of right or wrong. This is the moment when we are no longer in control of ourselves, the moment when anger emerges, leading to accusation, the moment for looking for ways to punish whoever we believe makes us suffer. Along with this angry mentality, physiological responses include noticeable changes ranging from red or pale face, heart palpitation, breathlessness, and high blood pressure, resulting in the inability to control ourselves.

This reaction will cause harm to us and to others, and we will no longer be capable of loving ourselves let alone loving others. Therefore, before we can love others, we must first know how to love ourselves. We have to be mindful of our daily material and spiritual consumption, in order to select what is beneficial to us and to others.

Introspection Generates Compassion

By looking within ourselves, we learn from our pain and suffering, from moments of anger and jealousy, and develop our innate wisdom and love. This process is like the lesson from those who, despite difficult episodes in life, can still have great love, because they know how to let go, and how to sympathize with and understand others. A good example is how parents sacrifice for their children. They deserve praise from poets and writers because, despite inconceivable hardship, they always show unconditional love for their children.

Therefore, looking within is an essential process in our daily activities. Do you ever listen to the whispering of your mind? Do you ever spend time observing your breathing in and breathing out, so indispensable to your life? Without breathing, everything you have built up in your entire life would be gone. So, one way to practice looking within is to sit down each day, following your breathing in and breathing out, and appreciating the presence of breath in the same way as you show your gratitude toward your mother who has nurtured you for years. Unfortunately, we usually take the importance of our breath for granted until the last day of our life when it is too late.

In short, "remembering ourselves," or turning inward, is the best method for achieving peace and freedom when facing conflict and difficult situations in life. When our mind is fresh and still, true loving-kindness will manifest. We then easily tolerate and forgive other people's shortcomings and mistakes. We can also easily let go of anger and aversion. Thus, our loving-kindness is enhanced through the process of "remembering ourselves" and bringing our body-mind to a state of unity, in order to clearly see reality as it is.

TAKING REFUGE IN THE DHARMA

Human beings must depend on each other to survive, to care and love each other, to share times of sorrow and joy in a changing world. However, depending on others or on external conditions only brings temporary happiness, as life is subject to impermanence, everything changes and will decay with time. Only taking refuge in the Dharma and in oneself will bring genuine happiness and peace.

When it came time for the Buddha's final passing and entering Nirvana, the Awakened One exhorted his disciples in the following way:

"Here, Ananda, now or after I am gone, be a Light unto yourselves, be an island unto yourself, a refuge unto yourselves, seeking no external refuge; with the Teaching (Dharma) as your Light, as your island, the Teaching as your refuge, seeking no other refuge. Those who, now or after I am gone, abide as an island unto themselves, as refuge unto themselves, having the Dharma as their island and refuge, it is they who will become the highest if they have the desire to learn." (PTS: Sanyutta-Nikaya V)

Since people cannot see their inherent happiness, they tend to depend on others to satisfy their greedy mind; they suffer if their expectations are not met. We all know that external factors are always temporary and illusory, and may cause pain and suffering, but we still want to depend on others to satisfy our desires due to our not knowing how to control the greedy self. Therefore, we end up being surrounded by grief and affliction, and peace and freedom will be absent. Taking refuge in the Dharma helps us clearly see the true nature of life, and to avoid the wrong view of those who live in illusion.

Dharma consists of the teachings of the Awakened One about truth, which are both practical and necessary for human life. Dharma can be compared to a torch shining light into the darkness to show us the road to peace and happiness. These teachings explain the mutual relationships of all things in the world. (This is because that is. This is not because that is not.) For example, if parents cultivate a virtuous lifestyle, their children and the other members of the family will all receive the merit. In the same way, if the children live in harmony, show respect to their elders and kindness to their younger siblings, and work hard to live in joy and happiness, the parents will ultimately have peace of mind.

However, such mutual relationships do not always occur as expected. From the Buddhist perspective, they evolve according to past actions and the law of causes and conditions. The meaning of this law is that if we create a good cause, despite many obstacles such as being harried by a powerful person, we will get a wholesome effect. With this understanding, we will stay calm and undisturbed when confronting unwanted events. All phenomena always operate according to the law of causes and conditions and the karma of each sentient being. They will manifest when favorable conditions come around. Therefore, we must just keep our mind clear and calm, free from anxiety, in order to live a good life, because happiness or suffering depends on our attitude in the present moment. With a grasping mind, always choosing and coveting, we will lose our freedom, and afflictions will manifest. If we always take refuge in the Buddha's teachings, the light of wisdom will always be shining to help us withdraw all the fetters of misery in this tumultuous life.

Taking refuge in the Dharma also refers to the practitioner who is able to see the true nature of all phenomena and to live fully in conformity to their manifestation. In other words, we must recognize the dynamics of all phenomena as they are, without any intention of grasping, rejecting, or discrimination. If we want to impose our subjective opinion or personal perception upon reality, we may be separated from its positive aspects, and our life will become as impotent as a cell separated from its body.

Dharma is also the truth, and the universal nature of life everywhere. It is the sun shining ubiquitously. You just open the door, then light will immediately come in; it is not necessary to look for the light elsewhere. You cannot use language or your subjective concepts to be in touch with reality; just let go of all concepts and you can see and feel reality as it is. The Buddha's teaching is just like a finger pointing to the moon. Following the direction of the finger enables you to see the moon without any additional explanations from others describing the moon. However, people are used to erroneously taking the finger for the moon. There is the false hope that relying on somebody else will bring long-lasting happiness. But the truth is otherwise; we must return to ourselves, taking refuge in ourselves, and dwell in our immediate reality to find a better way to freedom and happiness, without depending on anything or anybody.

Without mindfulness in our daily lives, the mind that craves and the habit of depending on others will emerge. The Exalted One added these teachings:

"Herein, Ananda, a Bhikkhu dwells contemplating the body in the body, earnestly, clearly, comprehending and mindful, after having overcome desire and sorrow in regard to the world; he dwells contemplating feeling in the feeling, mind in the mind, and mental objects in the mental objects, earnestly, clearly, comprehending and mindful, after overcoming desire and sorrow in regard to the world, then, truly, he is an island unto himself, a refuge unto himself, seeking no external refuge, having the Dharma as his island and refuge, seeking no other refuge."
(PTS: Sanyutta-Nikaya V)

Contemplating the body, feelings, mind-states and mental objects — practicing the Four Foundations of Mindfulness — is taking refuge in the Dharma, taking refuge in oneself. When standing, walking, sitting, or lying down, be clearly aware of progressive events with an honest and objective attitude, without acting from subjective thought. In the Shurangama Sutra, the Buddha taught: "A view formed by knowledge is the root of ignorance." In other words, judging a fact by the intervention of the self is the root of suffering.

According to the Buddha's teachings, no matter how much money, property, or fame we may possess, we still cannot enjoy full happiness because, as mentioned in the Diamond Sutra, "...the possession of attributes is an illusion." This means that whatever has form is an illusion, or all forms are illusory, because they will deteriorate with time. It is an indisputable fact. Indeed, the Dharma, and the island of the true self, are the places of everlasting peace for us to take refuge in. Therefore, the practitioner must clearly see this problem, and frequently look within to fully live in peace and freedom.

SHARING CONFIDENCES WITH A NOVICE MONASTIC

As a novice monk, you may be older than me. You may be very clever, talented in many realms. You may have been a teacher, or a noted doctor, or a CEO of a big corporation. Now, as a newly ordained monastic, you are my little brother or sister, an innocent child.

A person newly ordained is like newborn child who must go through many stages of practicing how to crawl, sit, stand, and walk; how to eat, talk, listen, and see. Thanks to this learning process, the sublime manner of a monk or nun progressively takes shape in a serene and virtuous environment. You would better not underestimate the importance of how you speak or walk; you may not even accomplish anything even after a lifetime of practice. Normally, you would not pay much attention to your manners in daily activities and would not be aware of your body-mind condition. Even you get distracted and lack enough concentration chanting the Buddha's names, reciting sutras, prostrating and meditating.

We usually live in illusion and shun reality. Our body is here, but our mind is elsewhere. We may be eating, but our mind is absorbed by the past or is gazing off in the future. Our mind is not present with our body to fully enjoy our food, being grateful to all species who help give us our daily meal.

Therefore, eating with mindful manners is also a part of practicing Dharma, alongside sutra recitation or Buddha-name invocation. A monk has the same duties as any ordinary person, including cooking, sweeping, dish washing, and watering the plants – but if he fulfills his duty with mindfulness, happiness is always there.

You should be aware that at the outset of life in a monastery, a novice's mind is like a wild garden where good and bad seeds are carelessly intermingled. Good communication, sharing joy, deep listening, and accepting others' limitations plant wholesome seeds. However, in our minds, there are also seeds of anger, jealousy rejection, laziness, blame, and ego, mixed with the good seeds. In ideal conditions, everything goes well. Living and working in favorable conditions, maintaining good relationships with others, the wholesome seeds will sprout and thrive. But in unpleasant or unwanted circumstances, bad manners and foul language will manifest. Therefore, a novice monk or nun must look for better ways to guide his/her mind in a positive direction. You should remember that your mind is a storage space, capable of receiving and retaining both good and bad things. You must not consume magazines, movies, and music with unhealthy contents. You must use your wits to choose only what is necessary for your training in the monastery.

Starting monastic life, you are guided by a master or a senior monk or nun as to how to learn and practice, from the basic to the higher levels of Buddhist teachings. You are not supposed to read sutras or textbooks not at your level of knowledge nor comment on others' achievements. A beginner with only basic Dharma knowledge and limited practice time is obviously not able to surmount daily hindrances and obstacles. He/she tends to be aloof when others commit errors or make mistakes. This is a quite common and dangerous attitude which a novice must seriously contemplate.

Being aware that as a novice monk/nun you will not receive many offerings, you would better not squander donations from your students. If you truly aspire for enlightenment and liberation, you must maintain a quite simple life, the way of life of self-contentment and minimal desire; whenever you have abundant comfort and luxury, selfishness and attachment will emerge, giving you little time and willingness to practice.

Every day, you must spend time to quietly ask yourself how much you have changed since you entered monastic life, as to your action, speech, and mind. Is your body more cautious in walking? Is your speech more compassionate? Are your understanding and your loving kindness growing? You must contemplate these matters daily.

To nurture your original pure mind and awakened wisdom, you have to maintain clarity in your actions, speech, and thoughts, observing your body and mind in present circumstances just as they are. Such insight is necessary in practicing Buddhism, as taught in the Sutra on the Four Foundations of Mindfulness. If you study and practice this sutra diligently, you will be liberated and attain enlightenment one day, which is precisely a monk's or nun's highest goal. It is also the way to return your master's favor and deserve the respect and offerings from Buddhist disciples.

THE TEACHER-STUDENT BOND

The relationship between a teacher and a student is one of the most precious and beautiful emotional ties and should be treasured and nurtured. An old Asian expression states, "One word is a teacher; half a word is also a teacher." This means you owe your teacher every word of what you have learned, and even half of that. This expression has a profound meaning, reminding the younger generation of the teacher-student bond and suggesting they express gratitude, respect, and humility toward their teachers. Regarding this topic, the Exalted One taught:

"There are five ways in which pupils should minister to their teacher. What five? By rising to greet them, by waiting on them, by being attentive, by serving them, and by mastering the skills they teach. And there are five ways in which their teachers, thus ministered by their students, will reciprocate. What five? They will give thorough instruction, make sure they have grasped what they should have duly grasped, give them a thorough grounding in all skills, recommend them to their friends and colleagues, and provide them with security in all directions." (Digna 31: Sigalovada Sutra, III)

This teaching reflects the Vietnamese tradition of respecting teachers and setting high esteem for religious paths. This spirit is found in the popular proverb: "When you drink, remember the source of the river; when you eat the fruit, think of the person who planted the tree." You must first learn from the teacher the moral values, and how to behave properly in society. You must also consider his health, his work and other needs related to his research in order to improve his teaching career. You should also show sincere and respectful manners. A simple material gift offering does not completely reflect the spirit of the above tradition.

Nowadays, there is no longer the real relationship between teacher and student as in the past. Perhaps, due to being accustomed to the complex human relations in a materially developed society where living standards are much higher, plus lack of time, teachers and students cannot maintain a warm relationship. This also occurs in spiritual or religious institutions where masters and disciples grow more distant from each other, resulting in a decrease of moral values and wholesome conduct, since disciples cannot inherit all the masters' valuable experiences. Due to this lack of knowledge and experience, when encountering difficult situations, the student is unable to overcome the greed, anger, and delusion hidden in his subconscious, and will be bound by affliction and sorrow. Therefore, sharing experience and knowledge with a master is the best way to remove these fetters and lead a leisurely, happy life.

To develop his inherently virtuous nature, the student must listen deeply in order to understand all the lessons transmitted by the teacher. He must always remember that by assimilating all the essential teachings, his thoughts, speech, and actions will reflect the wholesome aspects of the teacher-student relationship in social life and in the religious environment. Besides that, the student must be resolved to aim for a complete understanding and achievement, benefitting himself, his family, and his community. Gratitude is an important virtue in Asian culture. In the old days, according to Confucianism, the teacher is ranked above the father in the ranks of three most respectful people: king, teacher and father. Without respect for the teacher, no matter how successful the student is, he still does not fulfill a student's duty.

The Tathagata taught the teacher has five basic responsibilities toward the student. These responsibilities, if performed properly by the teacher, will be useful in transforming the student's hindrances and insecurity. Compared to the task of a schoolteacher, the responsibility of a master in a religious institution is much more difficult and requires a much higher standard. To transmit religious knowledge and methods of practice, the Buddhist master must teach a monk, through the nonverbal example of "body language," the noble manner for standing, walking, eating, and all other daily activities, and reflecting loving-kindness and compassion through his verbal teaching. Through this double task, the master provides a link to better education and improved spiritual development for future generations. Therefore, teaching is considered a very noble and well-respected profession.

The transmission of knowledge and moral values to the next generation eventually becomes the duty of the older generation. Therefore, teachers must guide students on how to find a stable career and to understand the true value of life, in order to be of benefit to their family and society. Each thought and action of the master is a valuable lesson helping his disciples carry on the work, heritage, and wisdom of the Ancestors and Bodhisattvas. Ideally, providing the best education, the teacher must be aware of the student's character, talent, and lifestyle in order to transmit all his knowledge and skills. This kind of teaching is like a physician giving each patient a particular medicine. From a higher level, a master must explain to the disciples the functioning of the interdependence between their body-mind and the world. From this perspective, the disciples will be able to obtain profound knowledge for all realms of life and transform affliction and suffering into joy and peace. However, this ideal aspiration also depends on the disciples' individual situation. Take as an example how falling rain covers the earth equally, but how much water is absorbed depends on the nature of the different kinds of plants and trees. The conscientious transmission of knowledge and experience from the master is obviously of indispensable value, but how much the disciple can assimilate is another matter, of no less importance. The real world shows us that lazy students who are not devoted to learning constitute a serious obstacle for the teaching profession.

After the student's successful graduation, a responsible teacher must offer recommendation and reference to future employers. On one hand, the student has the opportunity to serve society, and, on the other hand, he is able to continue in the teaching profession, transmitting knowledge to future generations. The teacher must favor the talent of each student, providing favorable conditions for their specialization and future research. In this way, the students will be of greater benefit to society, their nation, and the world. Then the teacher will be considered a success in achieving his educational task.

According to Buddhist philosophy, the body-mind of both the student and teacher must be fully and simultaneously present for each other, for the teacher-student relationship to be deep, pure, and beneficial to society. By returning to the present moment, the teacher will clearly see and understand the student's state of mind. His teaching will become more dynamic, effective, and helpful in the present moment. The same principle applies to the student, who also needs to return to himself, contemplating the state of his body-mind in the current situation, in order to gain valuable lessons from the teacher.

WISDOM IS SHINING

According to Buddhism, every sentient being has an inherently clear, pure mind. Since it is usually covered by the polluted world, that mind's original nature cannot yet manifest. The moonlight is always shining, but due to the clouds, everything is sunk in darkness; once the clouds disperse, the sky will clear. Similarly, once the light of wisdom shines, the darkness of ignorance will disappear. Then our true happiness will manifest and spread to our surroundings.

We regularly celebrate the Buddha's birthday, the day when Buddha appeared in this world to show the real value in life and the way to liberate all sentient beings from affliction and suffering. The image of a newborn Buddha is the symbol of wisdom emerging in our mind. The Tathagata said: "The Awakened One is a Buddha, all sentient beings are Buddhas-to-be." This means that all sentient beings have Buddha Nature. Everyone has the potential of attaining Enlightenment and becoming a Buddha. However, as we are bound to and controlled by greed, hatred, and delusion, this insight wisdom has no opportunity to manifest. Thanks to favorable conditions for understanding and practicing the Buddha's teachings, our mind can fully awaken, able to see the true nature of all phenomena in the world:

*"Light your lamp of wisdom,
And it will shine everywhere,
Guiding you through the Dharma.
There's no need to search for Nirvana elsewhere."*
(Thich Vien Ngo)

In fact, if we dwell in the darkness of ignorance and desire, we cannot see the dynamics of how all phenomena work, so we are easily manipulated and dominated by the self. When the light of wisdom is shining, peace and happiness will manifest naturally, without any need to looking for them elsewhere. Dominated by self, human beings must endure the pain and suffering of continually dying and being reborn in the cycle of samsara, with its six realms. Living in mindlessness, unaware of what we are doing, the egoic-self emerges, controlling all our activities, leading to a variety of afflictions for ourselves and others.

In Buddhism, to live in submission to the self is to go against life's natural conditions, including the law of cause-and-effect. The self is accustomed to selecting, grasping, and coveting what it wants, while life's reality is completely different. Aging and illness are facts of life, but people always expect youth and good health to last forever. This expectation is obviously impossible because it clearly goes against the laws of nature. Clouds leisurely float in the sky, the waters quietly flow to the sea, trees produce fruits that perish, as, eventually, will the trees, too. These changes are part of nature's cycles. Illness is a fact of life: fatigue and stress are results of overworking, and so good rest is necessary to restore good health. However, to satisfy the demands of the greedy ego, people refuse to listen to nature, and continue to work hard for more and more material comfort, leading to pain and suffering. According to Buddhism, all physical or mental phenomena must go with the flow of the law of causes and conditions, and every individual's action will create karma in the future life.

Therefore, one who lives in harmony with the laws of nature, without any intervention of self, deserves the Buddha's praise, as he said in his last instructions before his passing away:

"Here, Ananda, whatsoever monk, or layman or laywomen abides by the Teaching, lives uprightly in the Teaching, walks in the way of the Teaching, it is by him that the Tathagata is respected, venerated, esteemed, worshipped and honored in the highest degree. Therefore, Ananda, abide by the Teaching, live uprightly in the Teaching, walk in the way of the Teaching, thus you should train yourselves."

(PTS: Digha Nikaya I).

"Abide by the Teaching" refers to following the dynamics of how natural phenomena work, which means that we do not let our attention, opinion, knowledge, or concepts impose themselves on reality as it is. Whatever is happening, just look at that reality in order to act, and, once finished, let it go. A good example is our hands, which are capable of holding anything and doing all kinds of tasks, but, when their job is done, they no longer hold anything. Thus, the hand is capable of doing everything.

Once we experience every event happening in our body-mind fully, we will be able to clearly see the intention of self. Therefore, all conventional knowledge, rules and regulations, and patterns of reaction that have been fabricated for so long by self, will fade away in the shining light of the wisdom of non-self. The process of the fabrication of self is very cunning and subtle. If we lack awareness for only a moment, our thoughts, speech, and actions will be dominated by the self's craving, hatred, and delusion; thus, our action, whether big or small, will only serve the subtle, unwholesome intention of self.

The image of a newly born Buddha is a symbol of the selfless wisdom inherent inside of us. Whoever develops such wisdom will live uprightly in a continuously changing world, without being bound or dominated by any external condition or circumstance. Therefore, despite defilements, unwanted situations, obnoxious and polluted surroundings, we remain calm with a deliberate mind, capable of rescuing others from suffering.

To develop wisdom and live adapting to conditions, in conformity to the flow of the dynamics of all phenomena (teachings of the Dharma) in all circumstances, we must quietly observe their nature to arise and pass away, without our grasping or rejecting. In other words, we must not allow our ego to intervene and distort the reality of the here and now. Letting go of any perception or desire, even the noble aspiration to attain Enlightenment, is a necessary condition for wisdom to manifest, like a lantern shining light into a darkened room. With the presence of wisdom, in any place and at any moment, we will live spontaneously and peacefully.

DEEP LISTENING, THOROUGH UNDERSTANDING AND GREAT LOVE

Deep listening to others is extremely important in human relationships. Without paying attention to and proper consideration of what the other person says, dialogue will not be fruitful. You unintentionally limit your sympathy and compassion for others, and he or she will feel isolated and never want to share any important or secret thoughts with you. That is why it's so evident that deep listening is a necessary factor for mutual trust and understanding, which are at the foundation of love.

In the teachings of Mahayana Buddhism, many sutras such as the Lotus Sutra and the Shurangama Sutra refer to Avalokitesvara, the Bodhisattva with the great capacity of deep listening. The Bodhisattva of Great Compassion, Avalokitesvara is willing to listen to the cries of all sentient beings to rescue them from suffering and bring them joy. Whoever longs for peace and for elimination of bad karma can invoke the Bodhisattva's name, for liberation from adversity and suffering. Avalokitesvara Bodhisattva can appear in different forms ranging from a Buddha, a heavenly being, a human being, or an angry ghost, all for the purpose of teaching or saving life, at his discretion. His vow is that wherever there are sentient beings who ask for help, he will come to guide and transport them to the other shore.

In Buddhist tradition, Avalokitesvara Bodhisattva is the perfect symbol of the love and deep listening which is inherent in each of us. If you practice deep listening with compassion, without prejudice, or judgment, in order to understand other people's feelings, you will become a bodhisattva in the mundane world. Usually, we are easily bothered hearing someone using offensive language; we only want to hear someone who speaks pleasantly and genuinely. Listening with judgment and discrimination creates misunderstanding, and doubt among friends, and may lead to broken relationships.

In the Plum Village Chanting and Recitation Book, Zen Master Thich Nhat Hanh wrote a practical guide to practicing the virtue of Avalokitesvara Bodhisattva's deep listening:

"We invoke your name, Avalokitesvara. We aspire to learn your way of listening in order to relieve the suffering in the world. You know how to listen in order to understand. We invoke your name in order to practice listening with all our attention and open heartedness. We will sit and listen without any prejudice. We will sit and listen without any judging or reacting. We will sit and listen in order to understand. We will sit and listen so attentively that we will be able to hear what the other person is saying and what is being left unsaid. We know that just by listening deeply, we already alleviate a great deal of pain and suffering in the other person."

The meaning of this invocation is truly clear and certain. If we pay full attention during an on-going dialogue, not only can we understand what the other person is saying, but we are also able to understand what is yet unsaid. Then we will have a good chance to support and guide the other person towards the right direction, with a good, positive attitude. If we can cultivate such capacity of deep listening, we will develop understanding and compassionate love like Avalokitesvara Bodhisattva.

In fact, there are times we really do not listen with care to family members and friends. Before they can even finish a sentence, we cut them off, urgently blame, incriminate, or completely ignore them. Perhaps, due to our self-love, or to the fear of our pride being hurt, we exert ourselves to prevent someone from talking about the truth. Such behavior creates deep resentment in others and even in our own conscience. This harmful habit prevents us from listening deeply in order to understand and love other people who are facing difficulties and suffering. There is a Zen-flavored Vietnamese folksong, which can help listeners relax while, at the same time, releasing their worries and sorrow:

"If someone says something to you, listen to them,

Listen to them deeply, understand them thoroughly, and love them with a big heart.

What has bothered you over these days,
And made you look so gloomy?
Laugh it off, then breathe deeply,
And your sorrows will disperse in no time.

Tang tình, tang tính, tính tang
Tang tình, tang tính, tính tang."

When the song says, "If someone says something to you, listen to them," the verb "listen" does not mean to reluctantly listen, or listen in order to avoid hurting someone's feelings. It means to listen "as such", in and of itself – the kind of listening free from your likes or dislikes. It is a kind of listening free from your prejudices and your judgments of right or wrong, good or bad. If you can let go of those kinds of reaction, wisdom and compassion will gradually manifest and help you communicate with others with loving-kindness. To cultivate this capacity for deep listening, you must first look back within yourself, master your body and mind, and release your own suffering, before you can help others. The Tathagata taught:

"If anyone wants to hurt you
and pushes you into a great fire pit,
if you contemplate the power of Avalokitesvara
the fire pit will change into a pond.
If you drift upon the great ocean
and meet danger from dragons, fish, and demons by the waves,
if you contemplate the power of Avalokitesvara
you will not be swallowed by the waves.
If you are on the peak of Sumeru
and somebody pushes you,
if you contemplate the power of Avalokitesvara
you will remain in the air like the sun."

(Lotus Sutra, Chapter XXV) 117

Avalokitesvara, in this sutra, refers to awareness, which helps you to turn inward, to passively observe what is going on in your body-mind and in your present circumstances. When such mental formations as anger (fire pit), greed (ocean wave), and ego (peak of Sumeru) arise, you only need to contemplate their birth and death, their nature of coming and going, then they immediately vanish. As the above paragraph of the Lotus Sutra tells us, once you have awareness (by invoking Avalokitesvara's name), the self of greed, anger, and delusion, cannot control or tie you up, even when encountering unwanted situations.

    Finally, to cultivate the power of deep listening and the great compassion of Avalokitesvara Bodhisattva, you must first turn inward to clearly observe your mind along with the "arising-ceasing" cycle of all phenomena. Thus, you will be able to obtain better understanding and greater loving-kindness, leading to a peaceful and happy life for yourself and others.

WHOLE-HEARTED REPENTANCE

From time to time, human beings commit mistakes. Obviously, once our mind is deceived, any word and deed can easily hurt us and create suffering in others. Therefore, to feel remorseful or contrite for a past error and to promise oneself not to repeat that behavior, is honorable and universally respected. It sets an example for others to follow.

Repentance is a positive attitude, an orientation to a wholesome path, an acceptance of the truth, and an aspiration for personal transformation to a higher moral standard. In Buddhism, repentance is the elimination of the errors created by greed, hatred, and delusion, in order to purify the mind. There are two steps in the repentance process. The first part is to be rid of a mistake already committed; the second part is vowing to never repeat that mistake again and at the same time not to harm any sentient being. Thus, repentance is a necessary and concrete way to bring happiness to us and the world.

In real life, people commit serious mistakes, and there is no way to rescue them. They live in fear and anxiety, unable to eat or sleep, haunted by bad dreams. They are lonely regardless of their wealth since no one wants to be their friend. However, according to Buddhism, nothing is permanent. Even after committing unwholesome deeds, if we repent, have remorse and a determination to transform our bad karma, we are still able to become good people, rendering great service to our family and society. This kind of teaching about repentance is mentioned in the Majjhima Nikaya (Middle Length Discourses) in the story of how the Tathagata transformed an infamous killer into a monk.

Once, there was a young Brahmin student who became a highwayman. After he'd murdered people, he'd cut off the little fingers of his victims and string them into a necklace. For his growing garland of bloody fingers, he was nicknamed Angulimala, meaning "finger garland" or "finger necklace." One day, Angulimala spotted the Buddha walking along. At that time, he already had 999 little fingers around his neck. He needed only one more to reach his goal. He expected to easily catch the Buddha and quickly finish the job. Strangely enough, although the Buddha was only walking, serene and unhurried, Angulimala could not catch up with the Buddha even when running full speed. Eventually, he had to scream for the Buddha to stop. Turning around, the Buddha told Angulimala: "I have already stopped; now it is time for you to stop killing." Moved by the Buddha's words, he threw away his weapons and followed the Buddha back to the monastery, where he learned how to repent and later became a monk. He practiced the Dharma and attained Arahatship.

Nowadays, the world has plenty of crazy people spreading terror everywhere. Besides setting up funds to help victims of hurricane, earthquake, and tsunami, nations also invest a great deal of money to prevent and fight terrorism. If these terrorists, like Angulimala, threw down their weapons, practiced repentance, and returned to a wholesome life, human society would be much better off.

Whole-Hearted Repentance | 96

The Buddhist concept of wrongdoings and repentance is expressed in the following verse (gatha):

"All wrongdoings arise from the mind.
When the mind is purified, what trace of wrong is left?
After repentance, my heart is as light as the white clouds
that have always floated over the ancient forests in freedom."

The Tathagata taught:

"Monks, there are these two wise ones. What two? He who sees his own fault as such and he who pardons, as he should, the fault confessed by another. These are the two wise ones." (PTS: AN: Gradual Sayings: Vol. I, Chapter III)

In this world, except for the perfect Bodhisattvas, we all have shortcomings and make mistakes. The main thing is to feel contrite or concerned by a sense of guilt for one's wrongdoing and to promise oneself not to commit it again. One must vow to keep a pure heart, and refrain from committing even a small mistake. That is the behavior of a wise one.

"Don't dismiss a small mistake
as being not harmful.
One after another,
tiny drops will fill a big bucket."
(Dhammapada, verse 121)

However, many people lack such awareness. They do not want to repent and aspire for progress; they give in to circumstances. They ignore the law of cause and effect, that a bad cause sooner or later will produce a bad consequence. Even knowing that they may cause disaster for others, they remain indifferent to their bad actions until they suffer their consequences. Then they begin blaming destiny and asking for favors from God. On the other hand, other people repent by simply imploring deities and Bodhisattvas or some external power to help them escape from their error. These deluded actions may lead to more wrongdoings, and develop more greed, fear, and delusion.

As a matter of fact, to repent is not to ask for favors from or implore some superpower, but rather to be ashamed of ourselves after we did harm to others. Repentance should include an honest remorse and the willingness to correct our mistakes and misdeeds. To comply with Buddhist teachings on repentance, we must diligently always follow the Path, in our daily activities from eating, walking, sitting, washing the dishes, house cleaning, and driving, to chanting sutras or invoking Buddha's names. We should be aware of all our states of our mind, and their nature of arising and ceasing. Once our mind has been purified, thanks to constant awareness, we will be able to recognize wholesome and unwholesome mental formations, in order to focus our energy towards creating benefit for ourselves and for others. Practicing awareness also helps people repent properly, based on the impermanent nature of all physical and mental phenomena.

We highly believe that a cruel, unskillful individual can become a decent, virtuous person, if he or she is determined to overcome wrongdoings and to learn from the noble sages how to change his or her life towards a good, wholesome direction.

In order to become a decent person, we must repent by accomplishing concrete, good deeds. According to Buddhist tradition, we have to mobilize our energy into activities, that are beneficial to others, such as donating to the poor and the underprivileged, making offerings to temples, and revering the Three Jewels. Bringing joy to others is also a practice of repentance. But most important is being aware of every single action, at any moment of your life.

In Buddhism, making donations and offerings while practicing awareness is called "the dual practice of merit and wisdom." This reflects true repentance, that helps transform bad karma, cultivates positive seeds, and liberates us from all fetters, thus leading to a peaceful and joyful life.

TAKING REFUGE IN THE THREE JEWELS

According to the Buddha's teachings, no matter how wealthy you are, from time to time you will still feel lonely, sad, and unsatisfied – because, if you are dominated and controlled by anxiety, fear, grief, and hatred, you will never have peace and freedom, unless you take refuge in the Three Jewels.

Taking refuge in the Three Jewels means taking refuge in the Buddha, the Dharma, and the Sangha. Buddha is the one who has achieved perfect, spiritual Enlightenment, liberated from the cycle of birth and death (samsara). He has great compassion and supreme wisdom, and helps people transform delusion into enlightenment and attain a peaceful, happy life. Dharma refers to the Buddha's teachings. They are Truth, through which people can see the deep root of all phenomena and correct their wrong view in order to heal themselves and contribute to the welfare of society. Sangha is a group of at least four ordained monks and/or nuns living together in tranquility and harmony, manifesting a pure way of life. Their mission is to continue the Buddha's path of wisdom and compassion, transmitting the Dharma to all sentient beings through their knowledge and experience. Such a mission is truly noble and deserves our respect and generosity. Without the Sangha, people would not be able to fully understand the valuable and profound teachings of Sakyamuni, our Master. Due to this important role of the Sangha, the Tathagata taught:

"To whatever extent there are communities or groups, the Tathagata's Sangha of disciples is declared the best among them. Walking the Way well in the Exalted One's Order of discipline, walking uprightly, walking according to the Dharma Method, living with the Dharma teachings... his Sangha of the Blessed One's disciples is worthy of gifts, worthy of hospitality, worthy of offerings, worthy of reverential salutation, the unsurpassed field of merit for the world." (PTS: AN, Vol II, Chapter VI, ii (52).)

Thus, the Three Jewels are the symbol of supreme happiness, the solid, secure place for all sentient beings to take refuge in.

However quite a few people have taken refuge in the Three Jewels, and received the Five Precepts Training, at special temple ceremonies, but they still do not thoroughly understand the Dharma, due either to unfavorable external conditions or from their own lack of effort. Thus, they still lack a correct way of living based on the essence of the Buddha's teachings, which then leads them to persistent sorrow and misery. The ceremony for taking refuge in the Three Jewels is only a ritual, reflecting our decision to choose a good way of life, but it will be of no benefit unless we learn and apply the Buddha's teachings in our daily lives.

Some Buddhists may misunderstand that once they take refuge in a ceremony with a monk or nun, they are not supposed to look for another master or go to other temples or monasteries, even if they have not yet received adequate Dharma education and practice from their present master. Since Sangha refers to an association of at least four monks and/or nuns, anyone still has the right to find another Dharma teacher who can help one thoroughly understand and practice properly.

Furthermore, if you take refuge, receive a Dharma name, and visit a temple only occasionally, going there to pray to the Buddha for personal benefit, you unintentionally create bad karma for yourself and set a bad example for whomever else wants to take refuge in the Three Jewels. Buddhism is not a religion of praying for blessings and benefits. Instead, we follow the Path of the Buddha to find peace and happiness. Therefore, taking refuge in the Three Jewels requires a thorough understanding and a right view of all aspects of life.

It is good to learn the subtler meanings of taking refuge in the Three Jewels. For instance, Buddha represents wisdom: our taking refuge in Buddha also means that we are taking refuge in our own inherent wisdom. When our mind is clouded by desires, ignorance, and craving, then wisdom or "seeing things as they are" cannot manifest. So, in Buddhist tradition, my taking refuge in the Buddha also means taking refuge in the Buddha in myself. Likewise, since Dharma represents Truth, taking refuge in the Dharma also means taking refuge in the Dharma in myself. Since Sangha represents purity, taking refuge in the Sangha also means taking refuge in the Sangha in myself.

Therefore, to open the gates for wisdom to manifest, we must practice frequent introspection to see our body-mind state and our related circumstances. When your mind is still and clear, you will be able to understand the interdependent dynamics of all phenomena as such, and you can really take refuge in the Three Jewels. Otherwise, the self of greed, hatred, and delusion will control your mind, resulting in affliction and suffering. Formality and ritual are not the main parts of the practice of taking refuge; rather, we must learn how to contemplate our thoughts, speech, and actions in every moment. By whole-heartedly practicing the Dharma, we may reach a state of supreme happiness, so valuable that the Dharma is considered a jewel. Even the greatest treasure on earth is not capable of rescuing human beings from pain and suffering. Only taking refuge in the Three Jewels, turning our gaze back within ourselves, will lead to everlasting happiness.

Taking refuge in the Three Jewels also means you are walking the Buddha's path of understanding and loving-kindness. To do so, you must maintain your awareness in every step, at any moment, and in any place. You must thoroughly observe all your present-moment activities; in other words, you have to be aware of your body-mind state, just as it is, in relation to reality. For example, during yoga or martial arts practice, you must clearly recognize all your bodily movements, standing up, sitting down, turning around and back, and, at the same time, observe your breathing in and breathing out, for your practice to be fruitful. You can apply the same principle while driving, to avoid accidents; it is quite dangerous when your hands and eyes are in one place, but your mind is elsewhere.

Living in delusion, without awareness of reality creates suffering in ourselves and in others. Once the light of wisdom is shining in our mind, then our thoughts, speech, and actions will be of great benefit to ourselves and others. This is the noble, true meaning of taking refuge in the Three Jewels.

NO TIME FOR DHARMA PRACTICE

Almost every human being has to go through the same process of growing up, getting educated, working hard for a living, and contributing to a prosperous, civilized society. Whether through manual or intellectual work, each individual works industriously at their career, acquiring the material wealth necessary for personal needs. However, happiness will not be fulfilled if we do not have a spiritual life beside our material assets.

In terms of Buddhist beliefs, one must have a Dharma practice in order to attain true happiness. Yet people promise, "I will begin practicing after I have finished my job, or when I have free time." It may sound reasonable, but it is not true in real life. We may never finish our job because, after one project is done, another may follow soon after, unless we become so exhausted that we no longer can work. True happiness manifests only when our heart and mind are calm, clear, and pure, free from greed, hatred, and delusion. So, working for material needs must go along with spiritual practice.

People usually think that practice must be carried out in a temple, and then only chanting sutras and invoking Buddha's names, rather than a home practice. Others believe that spiritual practice is reserved only for the elderly, that young people must work until they have a stable career and will learn and practice Buddhism later on. In these ways, people unintentionally delay or limit their opportunities to practice by ignoring favorable conditions and circumstances. Actually, a temple is not the only place to practice Buddhism. You must first learn Buddha's teachings thoroughly and use appropriate methods of practice depending on different situations. Obviously, Buddhism is not a privilege of the elderly. It is for everybody, young and old, rich and poor, because all sentient beings are subject to greed, anger, jealousy, and envy. Everybody needs to learn Buddhism in order to transform unwholesome characteristics into wholesome ones, leading to a happy and joyful life.

The reality of our civilized world is that people of all ages suffer from pressure and stress. Students face pressure from competition at school; adults struggle daily in a fast change in todays' business environment, requiring constant updating of knowledge and information; company executive officers burden themselves with oscillating market prices, or bear responsibilities of saving a company in trouble. These are a few examples of a stressful way of life leading to fatigue, anxiety and depression, to the extent that people may commit suicide. The usual solution to de-stress is taking a vacation at a quiet, beautiful resort. In fact, vacation is only a temporary solution and cannot abolish the roots of affliction, greed, anger and ignorance; this is why once returning to daily duty, the previous deadlock and hindrances quickly reappear.

Time and circumstances are not a concern in practicing Buddhism; it is your perception that matters. Of the twenty-four hours in a day, scheduling a few hours of practice is obviously too little compared to time spent for sleeping, eating, and working. Look at the noble image of the great Masters who, once attaining Enlightenment, volunteered to return to the mundane world to help sentient beings learn Dharma. They went tirelessly from place to place to offer teachings, without wasting time, in their noble mission to help liberate people from suffering. With such a busy schedule, they continued to practice at any time and in any place, under any circumstances. The question is "Can we practice Buddhism that way?"

That question has been answered by the Tathagata in this Sutra:

"This is the sure way, monks, for the purification of beings, for overcoming sorrow and lamentation, for the destruction of suffering and grief, for reaching the right path, for the realization of Nirvana, namely The Four Foundations of Mindfulness. What four? Herein, a noble disciple lives contemplating the body in the body, ardent, clearly comprehending and mindful, having overcome covetousness and grief concerning the world. He lives contemplating the feelings in feelings, ardent, clearly comprehending and mindful, having overcome covetousness and grief concerning the world. He lives contemplating the mental-states in mental- states, ardent, clearly comprehending and mindful, having overcome covetousness and grief concerning the world. He lives contemplating the mental-objects in mental-objects, ardent, clearly comprehending and mindful, having overcome covetousness and grief concerning the world. And further, a noble disciple knows when he is going. 'I am going,' he knows when he is standing, 'I am standing'... And in going forward and backward, he applies clear comprehension; in looking straight on and looking away, in bending and in stretching out the limbs, he applies clear comprehension; in putting on the robe and carrying the bowl... he applies clear comprehension; in eating, drinking, chewing, and savoring, he applies clear comprehension; in attending to the call of nature, he applies clear comprehension; when walking, standing,

sitting, laying down, while falling asleep, in waking-up, when speaking or keeping silent, he applies clear comprehension and mindfulness."
(*The Four Foundation of Mindfulness: Majjhima Nikaya*) (*Sati = awareness*)

This teaching is very clear. We need to be aware of all activities of our body and mind and see clearly things as they are without likes or dislikes, without grasping or discriminating. This is the true way of practicing. The Buddhist teaching in the above-mentioned Sutra is also very pragmatic and concrete, helping us to flexibly apply our practice in any circumstance, and be free from any ritual.

The essence of the above Sutra focuses on three important factors: diligence, clarity and awareness. Diligence is an industrious, continuous effort to practice without neglecting the present moment. However, the correct diligence should exclude the hurried trend of satisfying a personal desire, even a noble aspiration for a status of peace and happiness, a desire that reflects our ego. We must clearly see the body-mind- circumstances as they are without prejudice, judgment and covetousness. Awareness is when we are present and see the reality as such. Therefore, diligence, clarity and awareness lead to a calm and pure mind without any intention to escape the negative aspect of the current circumstance or without being caught by the idea of coveting attractive objects. Coveting is the mind of craving and grasping while wishing to get rid of something is the mind of anger. The best way is to maintain a mere recognition of all phenomena in order to preserve peace and freedom.

The deep longing for love and for being loved is an important aspiration in human life. However, to satisfy this depends on whether we can accept the shortcomings of our beloved, and let go of "me" and "mine." In this way, true love will manifest. We may not need to waste time and effort looking for our beloved since he or she is already there, depending on our practice of the awareness of the here and now.

SEEING CLEARLY THE ILLUSORY SELF

Peace and true happiness exist only when our mind is free of the craving and grasping "self." That "self" is actually illusory. It creates an illusion. It tends to go against the unavoidable, natural dynamics of the law of causes and conditions. It wants to abolish what it dislikes, and to covet what it likes. It thus robs us of our independence and freedom. Failing to control our own mind results then in affliction and suffering. To liberate ourselves from the control of the false view created by the "self," we must see clearly its hidden intention as it creates mental formations and actions.

The worldly self clouds our mind to such an extent that we are unable to see reality for what it is. Here is the origin of various philosophical and theological doctrines which can lead to acrimonious disputes among proponents who cling firmly to their own view. Buddhism considers this as "self-view" and "self-grasping," a view created by an individual or group considering their concept as Truth, and which others must accept. Gradually, that view penetrates into their subconscious and quietly controls their mind.

Because of the worldly self, "I" and "mine" arise, along with "myself," creating a vicious cycle of craving, grasping, and becoming; samsara and suffering. Romantic love is a good example of this cycle. At first, you see and love a beautiful woman (craving), then you want her to be yours to satisfy your "self" (grasping, "mine"). You get her (becoming) because she accepts your love. The next scenario may be that she leaves you, hurting your pride and your ego (self), and you get angry and think about vengeance (hatred). An alternative scenario is that she agrees to stay with you, but you see her as so beautiful and you become so attached, that want to possess her forever (greed). You do not realize that impermanence is a fact of life (ignorance, delusion). When you lose her, you suffer. The beginning is a worldly self, the end result is suffering. As you do not see clearly what is arising in your mind, the formation of a "self" begins, and from there all your thoughts and actions are controlled by the "self." It wants to covet and grasp what is good, lovely, beautiful, and it wants to discard, destroy, or get away from what it does not like.

The worldly self forms in any moment you are not aware of your emerging perceptions, and it will control all your thoughts, speech, and actions. You tend to grasp, covet, and accumulate what you like, and to reject, exclude, abolish, or stay away from what you dislike. For example, a writer is overwhelmed with satisfaction and pride when his book is admired and valued by his readers. On the other hand, when they disregard or ignore him, he feels humiliated and angry. The "self" is very subtle and clever: if we are not calm and clear-minded enough to identify it, there is no way we can understand how it affects us.

Actually, if we know how to deeply investigate our body and mind and related circumstances, we will be able to realize that nothing is really "I" or "mine" (self), because all phenomena are impermanent, in and of themselves; they flow like water, uncatchable and immeasurable. All things depend on each other in order to manifest and have no separate "self." This is, because that is; this is not, because that is not. Nothing exists separately in the universe, because its nature is selfless and has a dependent origination. A flower is formed by a combination of several components which are of "non-flower" nature, such as earth, garbage, air, and sunlight. If conditions are met, the flower manifests; when the conditions are no longer favorable, the flower disappears. The flower does not have a separate "self" and belongs to no one. Here is the Buddha's teaching concerning the "non-self":

In Savathi... then the Exalted One said *"What is not of you? Brethren, put it away. Putting it away will be for your profit and welfare."*

"And what, brethren, is not of you? Body, brethren, is not of you. Put it away. Putting it away will be for your profit and welfare." "Feeling is not of you, perception, mental formations, consciousness are not of you. Put them away. Putting them away will be for your profit and welfare."

"Just as if, brethren, a man should gather, burn, or do what he pleases with all the grass, all the sticks, branches, and stalks in this Jeta Grove — pray would ye say "This man is gathering, burning us, doing what he pleases with us?" 'Surely not, Lord'. 'Why so?' Because, Lord, this is not our self, nor of the nature of self."

"Even so, brethren, body is not of you. Put it away. Putting it away will be for your profit and welfare. Feeling is not of you, perception, mental formations are not of you, nor consciousness. Put them away. Putting

HAPPINESS: A MATTER OF PERSPECTIVE

them away will be for your profit and welfare." (PTS: SN III: 4. On not yours 33(1)).

We are unable to keep our body forever, much less our material comfort, since our body must follow the unavoidable, natural process of birth, sickness, aging, and death. The five elements of human being — namely, form, perception, feeling, mental formations, consciousness — are always changing. Their long-term survival is impossible, and they cannot be kept by anyone. Only the "worldly self" wants to do otherwise. Therefore, this is what the Tathagata teaches:

"Bhikkhus, whenever there is an idea of self, there is an idea of what belongs to the self. When there is no idea of self, there is no idea of anything that belongs to the self. Self and what belongs to the self are two views that are based on trying to grasp things that cannot be grasped and to establish things that cannot be established. Such wrong perceptions cause us to be bound by internal knots that arise the moment we are caught by ideas that cannot be grasped or established and have no basis in reality. Do you see that there are wrong perceptions?"

The Buddha continued: *"If, when he considers the six bases for wrong views (form, perception, feeling, mental formations, consciousness, and the world), a Bhikkhu does not give rise to the idea of "I" or "mine," he is not caught in the chains of this life. Since he is not caught in the chains of this life, he has no fear. To have no fear is to arrive at Nirvana. Such person is no longer troubled by birth and death; the holy life has been lived, what needs to be done has been done; there will be no further births or deaths, and the truth of things as they are is known."*

(Thich Nhat Hanh: Discourse on Knowing the Better Way To Catch a Snake.)

If the construction of "I" is wrong, then our actions are also wrong. Because the "I" creates actions, we are easily misled, hanging on to "this" and getting rid of "that." Meanwhile, phenomena operate naturally and harmoniously. A young person will eventually age, get sick, and die; hunger and thirst force people to eat and drink; after rain, there will be a sunny sky. It is also true that the air is polluted by industrial debris, and global warming is the result of the burning of fossil fuel, deforestation, and other human causes. It is likely that natural disasters, earthquakes, floods, hurricanes, tsunamis, and droughts are happening more and more frequently as the result of human activities which disturb the natural dynamics of how the universe functions. The law of causality predicts the consequence of the "cause": human suffering is the effect of its own action directed by the worldly self. Letting go of that worldly self will help us pave the way to peace and liberation.

Putting away the worldly self is impossible if we try to use only our intellect, which may lead us into the trap of our "greedy self." The best way is simply and quietly contemplating the unimpeded nature of all phenomena to arise and pass away. The mere recognition of reality as it is helps us easily banish the worldly self and subsequently maintain a life of freedom and happiness.

LOOKING FOR OBJECTS OF LOVE AND COMPASSION

All human beings need to be loved and have someone to love. True love must be mutual and consistent. Without a beloved companion, life can be bland. Love is an extremely important goal for everyone.

Beauty, higher education, or social status are not adequate criteria in choosing a lover, if the one you love is not capable of understanding and agreeing with your lifestyle. No matter how beautiful, wealthy, and powerful your beloved may be, do not expect a good life together if you are not compatible with each other. So, it is hard to find the person you've always dreamed of, because nobody is perfect. Everybody has strengths and weaknesses, with moments of good or bad behavior. Expecting to meet a perfect companion is a source of affliction and sorrow. Therefore, we must learn how to return to our true selves and escape the unwholesome aspects of our mind. That is why the Buddha taught:

"Monks, I know not of any other single thing so intractable as an untamed mind. An untamed mind is indeed a thing intractable."
"Monks, I know not of any other single thing so tractable as a tamed mind. A tamed mind is indeed a thing tractable."
"Monks, the mind that is tamed, controlled, guarded and restrained conduces to great profit" (AN: Vol. I: Chapter IV: The Untamed)

Clearly, if we do not recognize and know how to tame and control our mind, then our thoughts, speech, and actions will be directed by the self of craving and grasping, and we will end up suffering in difficult situations. The reverse is true — when we regularly contemplate our body and mind, transforming our negative views and behavior into positive and wholesome ones, then we can bring peace and joy to the world.

Actually, when your mind is untamed and dominated by ambition, greed, and selfishness, it is impossible to live happily with the one you love, sharing good and bad times together. Usually, you tend to avoid or abandon the person who does not fit your lifestyle and look instead for a more compatible person. After falling passionately in love with a new person, you become anxious about losing him or her. Suffering and insecurity manifests in either case. Not everyone accepts that life is subject to change and impermanence; yet nothing, including love, can last forever. Our body and mind undergo the process of birth and death in every second, leading to aging and sickness.

Human beings often encounter unwished-for changes, such as loss of wealth, and broken relationships, plus other unexpected events such as natural disasters. With deep contemplation of these facts of life, we will be much better off, knowing less grief and sorrow when running into bad luck or unwanted circumstances.

Actually, true love may exist when we let go of the choosy self, the self that wants to covet this and repel that; we should release the discriminatory self and transform it into the self of compassionate love, because the nature of all phenomena (dharma) is non-discriminative, and without dualism, such as good versus bad. Due to mindlessness and delusion, human beings are haunted by sorrow, affliction, pain, and suffering.

Thus, the Sixth Patriarch Hui-neng, after hearing a phrase from the Diamond Sutra - *"a mind awakened without abiding in anything whatsoever"* - attained the Great Awakening and exclaimed:

"How amazing that the self-nature is originally pure. How amazing that the self-nature is unborn and undying.
How amazing that the self-nature is inherently complete.
How amazing that the self-nature neither moves nor stays.
How amazing that all dharmas come from this self-nature."

(The Platform Sutra)

According to Patriarch Hui-neng's wisdom, all physical and mental phenomena are inherently perfect. They are always operating according to the law of cause and effect, dependent on the condemnation or merit we create in this present life. They are inter-dependent. Rivers, clouds, plants, rain, and sunlight do not exist by themselves alone, but each is present in the other. They are mutually creating. They are without any independent self; there is no object for the self to attach to. This means that when our mind does not create the subject (the "I" or the self), the object (mine) cannot manifest. We then live in ease, with selfless altruism, according to our conditions and circumstances.

In Buddhism, to attain this way of life, we should be aware of reality without being controlled by the Three Poisons of greed, anger, and ignorance. Then we will know how to radically open our heart to accept and love others.

Looking For Objects Of Love and Compassion

Actually, we must take care of our own body and mind, knowing how to love ourselves, before we are able to thoroughly understand and love others. For example, when someone uses strong words against you, if you lack the ability to stay calm, to clearly find the deep root of the problem, you will either quickly react with anger or try to escape from the unwanted situation.

Therefore, you will lose an opportunity to learn a lesson from it, and your ability to accept the other person will be decreased. Thus, looking within, transforming bad seeds into good ones, and beginning anew are necessary steps for the development of wisdom in a spiritual life.

The deep longing for love and for being loved is an important aspiration in human life. However, to satisfy this depends on whether we can accept the shortcomings of our beloved and let go of "me" and "mine." In this way, true love will manifest. We may not need to waste time and effort looking for our beloved since he or she is already there, depending on our practice of the acceptance of "what is" in the here and now. Looking for a compatible companion is important because human beings need to be loved and have someone to love. True love must be mutual and consistent. Without a beloved companion, life can be bland at best and potentially tragic.

LEARNING DHARMA WITH AN OPEN MIND

The Buddha's teachings are suitable for any audience, regardless of age, level of knowledge, or social rank. For intellectuals, the Tathagata pointed out the truth of the moment rather than talk about theories. For common people, He gave simple and easy lectures, using images from daily life to elaborate on His teachings. The Tathagata had to use many skillful means to guide sentient beings toward the Truth of Life, due to different levels of knowledge. Today, disciples must first learn from good Dharma teachers or masters, to be able to understand and correctly apply the Buddha's teachings in daily activities. If we practice with a teacher of questionable competence, who may violate Dharma precepts, and is not capable of supporting and guiding us on the path of liberation, then our Dharma knowledge will be very limited. Next, our mind must be free from subjective views or previously acquired concepts. We must maintain an unbiased attitude and a clear mind to be able to discover and value the Dharma just as we must do for other cultures or traditions. A tender open-heartedness will permit wisdom and understanding to manifest easily.

Based on differences in circumstance, culture, and traditions of different countries, the Buddha lectured in different ways appropriate to the particular background of each. Buddhism, therefore, branched out into different traditions and practice methods. Although we have chosen a certain method to practice Dharma, we still should learn and understand Dharma practice methods from other traditions so as to broaden our knowledge. If we are not exposed to other traditions, we will be subjected to a grasping ego (attachment to self) and clinging to the Dharma. If we pretend we have already acquired the most profound knowledge, even the most correct method of practice can be one of the greatest hindrances for Dharma practice.

Perhaps being unsatisfied in his aspiration for truth and enlightenment, Prince Siddhartha left his guru Udaka to continue his journey in search of the path to liberation. If he had chosen to stay with Udaka, who entrusted Siddhartha as leader of his spiritual community, he would not have become a perfectly awakened Buddha. Actually, a Dharma student often faces temptations from material comforts and joyful feelings arising from meditation practice. If we lack vigilance or are not properly guided by a good master, we will be trapped by the subtle self of greed, anger, and ignorance. When a practitioner lacks appropriate training and wants to remain for a long time in a comfortable place, he will be subject to the grasping mind and cling to material comfort. For this reason, the Exalted One taught:

"Monks, there are five disadvantages from staying too long in a place. What five? Many belongings and their amassing; much medicine and its amassing, many duties and things to be done and their concern; one lives with householders and wanderers, mixing with them, not averse from laymen's company, when one leaves that place, one leaves it with regret.

Monks, these are the five disadvantages..." (PTS: AN, Vol. III iii223: Staying too long.)

HAPPINESS: A MATTER OF PERSPECTIVE

The supreme goal of a Dharma practitioner is liberation and Enlightenment. The profound meaning of liberation refers to an unbound mind, free from any attachment, including the attachment to the concept of Nirvana. Therefore, the practitioner must always contemplate deeply the process of learning and cultivation. He should not get attached to material comforts, nor to offerings from disciples. As such, when he changes residence, his mind will stay free. A practitioner looking for a path to liberation will maintain a calm, leisurely lifestyle, and will not cling to the material world. His ideal of becoming an ordained monastic will be realized, his pain and suffering will be overcome, and his ability to rescue sentient beings will be worthy of the respect of human and heavenly beings.

To carry out this ideal requires the practitioner to have a clear, impartial mind. He or she must accomplish many good deeds, such as making donations and offerings to the Three Jewels, building temples and stupas, casting bells, printing sutras, and numerous other contributions. Even if these offerings may be as great as those of Emperor Wu Liang in Chinese history, his merits will be of little or no value if he keeps requesting his name and contributions to be remembered, and the recipients be grateful, for the sake of his fame and self-satisfaction. It is a big mistake for any practitioner who has reached a high level of practice — diligently meditating, prostrating, chanting sutras, invoking Buddha-names — to still firmly cling to and overestimate his own method and criticize other sects or methods. The supreme state of awakening and liberation is "no mind" (a mind free of all attachments, a busyness-free mind, a mind free from worries)

Many people misunderstand "no mind." They try to either maintain a blank mind, or a wandering mind, or a mind caring about nothing. Some, believing that they have reached inner calm and freedom, act like a "person who is completely undisturbed in the crowded market." "No mind" is neither a mind full of strategies and plots fabricated by the greedy self, nor a dull and deluded mind. Instead "no mind" is an undisturbed mind, unified-with no subject or object, that "shines the light of wisdom once the mind is empty." Thus, "no mind" refers to a transcendent mind with no intention of controlling or satisfying the greedy self. No effort is needed to find or to calm the worldly mind. All that is required is the inner silence of wordless awareness. "No mind" is the essence of Dharma learning, as expressed in Zen poetry:

"Dealing with all matters without false mind, no need to ask about Zen."
*(Vietnamese King and Zen Master **Trần Nhân Tông**)*

"When no mind arises in the presence of things,
Then no questions on Dharma is required."
(Zen master Huong Hai)

Constant insight into our thoughts, speech, and actions at any time and in any place helps us maintain a peaceful, free life. Our ability to passively observe all phenomena awakens the light of wisdom; then a craving, grasping mind will have no opportunity to emerge. Our view will begin anew, with more peace and clarity. At the same time, our behavior will show more flexibility and creativity in all our daily activities. And we are able to maintain our peaceful, leisurely life regardless of whatever unwanted situations we might encounter.

NO BLAME TO ANYONE

When something bad happens, we usually try to blame somebody else rather than find out what the deep root of the problem is. As we often react to whatever is bad for us, we also try to protect our prestige and honor, and assume that we are more knowledgeable than others. We hastily blame other people without listening to any explanation. Such an impatient attitude causes insecurity and misery to ourselves and others.

According to the Buddha's wisdom, problems in our daily life are the result of many complex factors. This is called the law of dependent origination. There is no single thing that creates the whole universe; rather, everything must depend on each other to manifest. "This is because that is, this is not because that is not; this arises because that arises; this perishes because that perishes." There is the rice plant because there is the grain, and vice versa. The grain and the plant have a mutual relation: each cannot exist separately without the other. Besides, the rice plant, by itself, cannot produce the grain; such production also depends on earth, water, air, and sunlight. This is a chain of factors based upon the mutual relation and inter being of all things in the universe. Contemplation and insight are necessary to discover this wonderful truth. If we thoroughly understand this principle, we will not lay all the blame on any one.

Not many people see and understand this wisdom. In normal human relations, people often fail to recognize their own mistakes, and blame others whenever they encounter obstacles or failures. We firmly assume that we are always right, and tend to ignore other people's opinion in solving problems, which can lead to discord and heated dispute. Overly proud, we ignore the fact that all created goods are the result of the toil of many people. How can a company operate without the help of its administrative assistants, janitorial team, and security guards? In other words, the director is not the only person responsible for his company's success. The director must realize that all employees' opinions and efforts should be considered and honored. Conversely, in case of failure, he won't be the only one to blame. Thus, we see that all things and phenomena have a very close mutual relationship. The Exalted One has taught this fact of life:

"Herein, brethren, two matted reeds lean against each other, if this one is pulled aside, the other will fall down; if the other is pulled aside, this one will fall down." (PTS: SN: Vol. II)

In fact, all sentient beings in this world must depend on each other to survive and flourish, as in the example of two bunches of reeds. A company will appreciate the efforts of the whole staff; a clever leader must avoid dictatorial behavior, emphasize the importance of the role of others, listen deeply to the employees, and create a warm workplace environment.

Following these guidelines will contribute to higher enthusiasm among employees and further ensure the company's success. This is a practical way of life as taught by the Exalted One.

When Ananda recognized the depth of causal law and declared it as being as ever so plain, the Exalted One taught:

"Say not so, Ananda. Deep indeed is this causal law, and deep indeed it appears. It is through not knowing, not understanding, not penetrating, that doctrine, that this generation has become entangled like a ball of string, and covered with blight, like unto Munja grass and rushes, unable to overpass the doom of the Waste, the Woeful Way, the Downfall, the Constant Faring On." (SN, Nidana-vagga; 60 (10) The Base)

Living in accordance with the principle of dependent origination is to live in happiness without hatred or grief. However, not everyone agrees with that principle; people still want to obey the worldly self of greed, hatred, and ignorance. They long for fame and social status, wish to be appreciated, respected, and admired, in order to satisfy the craving self. In Buddhism, this is the mindless way of life, lacking the awareness of seeing things as they are, leading, of course, to a "mind entangled like a ball of strings or shut off like a cocoon." Once the mind is clouded by delusion and craving, our view and wisdom will be limited. Our self-confidence and ability to handle difficult situations will be gone.

According to the Buddha's teachings, not a single thing can create any other single thing; anger or grief are no exception. Based on the law of dependent origination, when someone insults you, it is better not to blame him. You should recognize that, along with any harsh judgment, there would be not one but many factors which, according to the law of causes and conditions, are mutually operating and converging. Their bad behavior may have originated from their parents, other family members, or friends, who planted unwholesome seeds in them and watered them daily. With deeper insight, you may discover that the one who insults you is a victim of some misfortune or subject to several unfortunate situations such as poor upbringing without any chance to learn morality or ethics. It might well turn out that you would do better to love, help, and rescue them, rather than blame them. In fact, anger or grief are also a matter of perspective. Two different persons may hear the same strong words: the one who understands and practices the principle of dependent origination is at peace, while the other, without this understanding, may join with other people in strong action to harm their "enemy." The latter behavior brings no benefit to either side; on the contrary, it will only create bad karma. This is well explained in the Buddha's teaching:

"An eye for an eye will make both sides blind.
Let compassion prevail over revenge,
and you will have lasting peace and happiness."

Letting compassion prevail over revenge is not an easy practice. We must keep our heart and mind as clear as a mirror and turn inwardly in order to see clearly reality as it is, not as it will be nor should be. "Will be" implies the future, and "should be" reflects a restless self which expects everything to satisfy its appetite. The latter is a very bad habit, and a serious human disease. To abolish this harmful habit requires uninterrupted awareness as to the reality of the present moment, often referred to in Zen: "If the mind is in perfect awareness, the light of wisdom will shine." Just like the mirror, if it remains still, without dust, it will reflect an image just as it is.

Such a calm and clear mind is able to see the innumerable causes and arising conditions of each phenomenon in the universe. From there, our view is beyond space and time without clinging to any doctrine or philosophy. We are free to discover the wonders of life in the present moment. Therefore, with love and compassion, a Buddhist can see the shortcomings or misdeeds of others as a result of multiple causes and conditions and, of course, will not attribute any blame to anyone.

AS KIND AS A BUDDHA

Vietnamese people say "as kind as a Buddha" about someone who is gentle and likable, and does not fret or try to justify themselves if they are being scolded or slandered. That expression reflects the truth that there are people in this world with good hearts who are as tolerant and kind as a Buddha.

The expression "as kind as a Buddha" does not refer to a naive or insensitive person. Rather, he maintains an ordinary life with episodes of joy and sorrow, love and hatred. He knows that a verbal "tit for tat" brings nobody happiness but instead only creates discord, separation, and misery. He avoids futile dispute and self-justification. Instead, he listens deeply to sympathize with and understand others. He tries to maintain good social relations and develop noble qualities, to be passed down to future generations.

However, not everyone can follow such an example of perfect behavior. Being scolded, they quickly react sharply, vindicating themselves or temporarily avoiding unwanted situations, rather than remaining calm. Such behavior is far from that which brings true happiness. As disciples of Buddha, we must take His compassionate image as our model. Hot temper and greed do not reflect Buddhist behavior. Disregarding those who go to the temple only to pray for blessings and business success but don't study Dharma — Buddhist practitioners, who have taken refuge in the Three Jewels and been educated by the Sangha, must constantly cultivate right view and a clear mind. Of course, greed, hatred and selfish behavior often dominate the human mind; but once we have chosen to follow the path of the Tathagata, we must recognize our shortcomings and gradually acquire virtuous conduct, that will also generate peaceful energy in others.

The expression "as kind as Buddha" appears very early in Vietnamese folklore. Scholars of Vietnamese history confirm that in the First Century, Vietnamese people already called Buddha by the name "Bụt." Popular songs, proverbs, and fairy tales also used the term "Bụt." The Buddha pervades Vietnamese folklore, ranging from proverbs, such as "When with a Buddha, he puts on a monk's robe, when with a ghost, he dons a paper dress" ("Đi với Bụt mặc áo cà sa, đi với ma mặc áo giấy"), equivalent to "When in Rome, do as the Romans do," or "As beautiful as a fairy, and as kind as a Buddha" ("Đẹp như Tiên, hiền như Bụt") – to stories in which the Buddha figures, such as "The Story of Tấm and Cám," "The Bamboo Tree with a Hundred Nodes" ("Cây tre trăm đốt"), and "The Simpleton" ("Thằng Bờm").

Later on, influenced by Chinese culture and literature, Vietnamese people used the term "Phật" for Buddha. As a phonetic transcription of the Sanskrit "Buddha" into Chinese, the word "Phật" refers to a human being Completely Awakened, or Enlightened. Such a person is free from the Three Poisons of greed, anger, and ignorance. He has great compassion and wisdom in teaching sentient beings, and in helping them escape suffering and attain peace and liberation.

The Buddha has inconceivable loving-kindness, that is even greater than the love of a mother for her baby. The ability of listening deeply to thoroughly understand is inherent in anyone with such loving-kindness, as taught by the Exalted One:

"At any time, walking, standing, sitting, laying down, as long as still awake, one vows to being mindful of loving-kindness. This is the noblest way of life. Do not get lost in a false view, try to repel greed, and follow a healthy lifestyle and attain wisdom, as such, the practitioner will go beyond birth and death."

(Plum Village Chanting and Recitation Book)

Indeed, loving-kindness manifests when we live in mindfulness, that is, when we are aware of what is happening in the here and now. For example, when we drive, to avoid accidents, we must be fully aware of our body and mind in the current situation. Being aware of each thought and action is necessary for nurturing compassion and developing the inherent seeds of wisdom.

Taking refuge in the Three Jewels and having Buddha as our Master are our greatest blessings. Many people, due to unwanted circumstances such as economic hardships, never get a chance to learn and practice Buddhism. On the other hand, other people might have excess wealth and material comfort but are unconcerned about spiritual life. Who would have the courage to leave the royal palace to become a monk like King **Trần Nhân Tông** in Vietnamese history? A Buddhist living in wholesome conditions must vow to learn and practice the Dharma, without wasting time in gossip or useless debate. Furthermore, when our mind is not yet stable or fully at peace, we had best limit or avoid our contact with people or situations that are unfavorable to our practice. Due to a lack of mindfulness, along with a habit of procrastinating in learning, and without help from Dharma friends, a practitioner will have a hard time transforming his dangerous behavior. To help us repel bad habits and cultivate noble qualities, the Exalted One taught:

"Monks, if a monk follows six things, he will live here and now in great happiness and contentment, and for him the mold has begun to form for destroying the cankers. What six?

Herein, a monk delight in Dharma, in growth, in renunciation, in solitude, in being free of ill will and in non-diffuseness.

Monks, if a monk follows these six, he will live in great happiness." (PTS: AN: Vol III; iv (78). Happiness; Translated by B.M. Hare)

Quite a few people act out from their habitual programming, fabricated by their greedy, angry, and deluded ego, rather than shine the light of wisdom to overcome temptations and sensual desires. Therefore, with a mind of delight in the Dharma, studying and practicing "with renunciation, solitude, freedom from anger and useless debate," – the practitioner will be able to extinguish the fires of affliction and desire, eliminate all unwholesome seeds, and attain peace and freedom in this life.

As disciples of the Tathagata, we must follow His path, that helps us to develop understanding and compassion. We must improve our daily practice of mindfulness and awareness, in order to acquire a pure and clear mind and the energy of loving-kindness, that can be transmitted to others. As such, our speech and action will reflect a serene and calm attitude. People with such power of love are considered "as kind as a Buddha."

HONORING THE BUDDHA

Invoking or reciting the Buddhas' names, also known as Paying tribute to the Buddha, is one of the most effective methods of practice to transform suffering into peace, joy, and liberation for all human beings. However, it is not easy to achieve this goal unless the practitioner understands the core content of this method and applies it properly in daily life.

Invoking the Buddhas' names consists not only of a mere recitation of a certain Buddha's name, but it requires the inherent Buddha nature (loving- kindness and wisdom) be manifested in our daily lives. If, while reciting the Buddhas' names, one's mind is still scattered with grief, anger, jealousy, dispute, and insecurity, one cannot properly practice Buddha-recitation. Since the Buddha is the One Who Is Aware, enlightened, free of ill will, greed, and delusion, the practitioner of recitation must also maintain a mindful lifestyle and good ethical conduct, reflecting such virtues as understanding, love, sympathy, tolerance, altruism, and kindness. One's mind should be free from hatred and blame. One should not even flee from a dangerous situation but, on the contrary, remain there to listen deeply in order to develop understanding and compassion.

Awareness means centering our body and mind in the present moment without looking to an undetermined future or being bound by something off in the past. The Vietnamese words "niệm Phật" (honoring the Buddha) includes a phonetic transcription of the Chinese written word (念, niệm) which consists of the combination of the words "tâm" heart (or mind) and "kim" (present, now). Thus, "**niệm**" means the mind is here and now and not in another place or time. In other words, Buddha-name (recitation) allows us to look within ourself to live fully in the present moment.

The human mind is usually dominated by aspirations and ambitions. It remembers the past and dreams of the future. It rarely stops and contemplates itself so as to cultivate wholesome seeds and transform unwholesome seeds into wholesome ones. When unwholesome thoughts arises, without a calm and pure mind, we will create suffering in ourselves and others with our deluded thoughts, speech and actions. Regarding the role of the mind, the Exalted One taught:

"All mental phenomena have mind as their forerunner. They have mind as their chief. If with a polluted mind one speaks or acts, then suffering follows him, just as the wheel follows the footprint of the ox that draws the cart." (Dhammapada, Verse 1)

It is very clear that speech and actions are implemented through the guidance and control of the mind. With an unwholesome mind, bad speech and actions certainly will follow, just like the cart drawn by the ox. Therefore, we must recognize, regulate, and control our mind, and cultivate kind speech and good behavior, in order to live in peace and harmony with others.

To attain this goal, we must choose an appropriate Dharma method to practice. The following is one of the best and most miraculous of methods taught by the Exalted One:

"Monk, there is one thing which, if practiced and made much of, conduces to a mind that is well directed, to downright revulsion and disgust, to ending, tranquility, full comprehension, to perfect enlightenment,

to Nirvana. What is the one thing? It is calling to mind the Buddha. If practiced this one thing, Monks, it conduces to a mind that is well directed, to downright revulsion and disgust, to ending, tranquility, full comprehension, to perfect enlightenment, to Nirvana." (PTS: AN: Vol. I; 1-10, The One Thing)

As previously mentioned, Buddha-name invocation is to center attention of the body and mind within reality as such; in other words, we must be constantly aware of every thought, speech, and action. Since human beings often have mistaken perceptions and a diffuse and scattered mind, the purpose of the recitation of the Buddhas' names is to assist us in returning to mindfulness and awareness. While reciting the names of Sakyamuni Buddha, or Medicine Buddha, or Amitabha Buddha, if our mind does not let go these so called "illusory thoughts", our practice won't be effective.

Actually, the object of recitation is not limited to the Buddha's names; it may be recitation of Dharma, Sangha, precepts, dana (generosity), deities, and even recitation of the in-breath and the out-breath. All these different kinds of remembrance require continued awareness of their objects. The mind and its objects of contemplation are not two different entities. Remembrance is remembrance, breath is breath, there is no external self to control us, to set goals, to like or dislike, as taught by the Tathagata about "well-directed revulsion and disgust, ending, tranquility, full comprehension, and Nirvana." Thus, invoking the Buddhas' names is to let go of the self for the enlightened mind of Amitabha to manifest; in other words, when the self vanishes, the Pure Land will appear.

Quite a few people who invoke Amitabha Buddha's name can attain an undisturbed unified mind, have a pure and peaceful life, and acquire the ability to control their mind in the moment of death, and hence will be reborn in a corresponding peaceful realm. However, due to a busy social life or economic hardship, many people are not so diligent in their spiritual practice. Others promise to practice only after certain worldly goals are achieved; due to this misperception, they are not mentally prepared for a clear, calm attitude, so that when confronting obstacles in life, they cannot transform suffering into happiness. In fact, we should have joy all throughout our practice. Postponing the practice means delaying the inherent happiness inside each of us. We should be aware that life is short and impermanent and, no matter what we expect, we can never finish our tasks.

Actually, peace and liberation manifest only when our heart and mind are truly tranquil and pure. Our inherent Buddha nature is often clouded by a diffuse and scattered mind. Thus, people mumble the Buddhas' names but if they are not fully conscious of what they are reciting, they will get nowhere and achieve nothing. Amitabha Buddha is the One of Infinite Light, Endless Life, and Boundless Merit. So reciting Amitabha Buddha's name is actually a way to attain wisdom and a free, clear mind (infinite light), that shines light uninterruptedly (endless light). If your mind no longer has anger, hatred, and ignorance, and you live in reality as it is, your actions will bring inconceivable benefits, peace, and joy to all sentient beings (boundless merit).

People in modern society are faced with numerous complicated problems related to education, work, family, health, the economy, the cost of living, etc. and so may be subject to stress and mental disorders. In developed countries, material comfort alone is obviously not able to treat and heal various complex physical and mental illnesses. Fortunately, quite a few people have opportunities to learn and practice Buddhism, such as chanting sutras, invoking the Buddhas' names, and meditating. In so doing, their mind gradually becomes clear, leading to a peaceful and happy life.

Everyone has inherent Buddha nature. Dharma practice enables it to manifest. One of the most important conditions for shining the light of wisdom (Buddha nature) is to practice mindfulness and awareness continuously. This practice is not limited to reciting the Buddhas' names, chanting sutras, or meditating, but also includes gaining insight again and again into all personal activities such as standing, walking, sitting, lying down, driving, cleaning, cooking, bathing, combing hair, or washing dishes – recognizing the dynamic manner of their arising and passing away (birth and death). This insight helps us acquire tranquility, clarity and have mastery over our body and mind anywhere and anytime. This practice is really the work of Buddha-recitation for whomever who wants to walk the path of liberation.

AWARENESS OF BODY AND MIND

"With full awareness of body and mind
Listen deeply to each breath of yours,
Inside and outside of you
Dharmas remain as they are
And the mind is at peace.
What needs to be done is done."

(Thích Viên Ngộ)

Contemplating or being aware of body and mind is essential practice for any Buddhist walking the path of liberation. The human mind is always scattered by constant thinking and speculation. It is rare to find body, mind, and the external objects of mind all coexisting together. Most of the time, our body is in one place and our mind is in another place; thus, we lack the tranquility and clarity to understand our true nature and its ever-changing pattern, the ups and downs of human existence. So deep contemplation and passive awareness of body and mind can help awaken our inherent Buddha nature, clarify the inter-connectedness of all phenomena, and eliminate negative and unwholesome thoughts and actions.

However, not everybody knows how to recognize and master his or her mind, staying calm when facing life's changes. Human habits of wants and needs, along with the five sensual desires (fortune, fame, beauty, good food, leisure time) have accumulated in us during innumerable past lives.

They are so deeply ingrained that even when we try to show no desire, we still aspire for a calm, peaceful mind. Understanding that life is subject to pain and suffering, one searches for a spiritual life and diligently practices in order to attain enlightenment and liberation. At first, this sounds reasonable; but in reality, to dislike the present and to look for a better future, is in itself desire, which prevents enlightenment and liberation. To reject what we dislike in the present is the mind of anger. To cling to what we like or aspire for some goal in the future is the mind of greed. As long as greed and anger still dominate our mind, we are not able to attain liberation and enlightenment. Liberation refers to a mind that is not tied up by any concept, or in Buddhist terms a non-abiding mind. However, we often find peace and happiness through grief and pain because "affliction is the other side of enlightenment." So if we are resolved to eliminate all afflictions, we will not be able to attain an enlightened mind. Awakening does not mean seeking for perfection or mental satisfaction, because the more we look for perfection, the more we will be disappointed. Enlightenment, therefore, is to recognize and accept the imperfect nature of life.

In reality, we rarely have insight into the opposing aspects of human life: success and failure, winning and losing, wholesome and unwholesome, right and wrong. We tend to only see things subjectively, in a simplistic way or as controlled by our emotions. When we see a beautiful person, love arises and covetousness follows; when we hear an offensive voice, hatred and anger emerge and we want to stay away from the annoying circumstance. Such reaction obstructs our inherent good nature, leading instead to discriminating between grasping and rejecting. This discrimination is a source of everlasting suffering. Therefore, we must continuously recognize, control, and cultivate our own mind and thought in order to live in peace and freedom and to be potentially beneficial to others. Regarding this practice, the Exalted One taught:

"Monks, I know not of any other single thing so conducive to great loss as the untamed mind. The untamed mind indeed conduces to great loss."

"Monks, I know not of any other single thing so conducive to great profit as the tamed mind. The tamed mind indeed conduces to great profit." (PTS: AN: Vol. I; Chapter IV; 1-10)

The untamed mind is a wandering mind, the one that regrets the past, dreams of the future, and clings to the present; a mind that makes us lose our freedom and the ability to control our emotions. With that mind, when we encounter a difficult situation beyond our expectation, we will be easily influenced and controlled by the circumstances, resulting in poor decisions.

To tame the mind is to see clearly the dynamics of the arising and passing away of our feelings through passive observation or wordless awareness. Whenever a feeling like sorrow emerges, try to simply recognize it as it is, see it as it is, hear it as it is, know it as it is, without labeling it, or any judgement or intention of suppressing or destroying it. In this way, sorrow or other emotions will dissolve by themselves. If we are impatient in trying to eradicate afflictions, we will be trapped by the subtle mind of greed or anger, resulting in a perpetual vicious cycle of grief and suffering. Hence, this warning by Zen master Thien Lao: "Above the head is another head; a layer of dew is added on top of the snow."

We usually talk about the two foundations for contemplation, body and mind. Actually, we only need to see the "arising-vanishing" process of the mind – then, at the same time, we can clearly see all our body movements, and vice versa. The Exalted One in the Sutra on the Four Foundations of Mindfulness taught:

"Herein, a Bhikkhu in going forward and backward, he applies clear comprehension, in looking straight on or looking away, in bending in and stretching out the limbs, he applies clear comprehension; in putting on the robe and carrying the bowl, in eating, drinking, chewing and savoring, he applies clear comprehension and mindfulness; in attending to the call of nature, when walking, standing, sitting, lying down, when falling asleep, when waking up, when speaking or keeping silent... he applies clear comprehension and mindfulness." (MN: Vol. I)

A full understanding of what we are doing is to clearly see current reality, current bodily activities, seeing them as they are without the control of a greedy self (judgement).

In the Sutra on the Four Foundations of Mindfulness, the practitioner learns about four different aspects of contemplation: body, feeling, mind, and objects of mind. Actually, the practitioner needs to fully contemplate only one aspect: he or she will also come to understand the other aspects because the body, feelings, mind, and objects of mine are interrelated. For example, when we hear an unbearably disturbing noise, the mind immediately feels uncomfortable, then anger arises against the one making that noise; so it is very clear that a close, causal relationship exists between the body, the mind, and the object of the mind, a relationship that creates the multiple aspects of human life.

Nowadays, monks at some Buddhist centers in Sri Lanka, Thailand, and Myanmar practice only contemplation of the body without mentioning the three other aspects. This method brings real peace and happiness and attracts numerous practitioners around the world. Buddhists in Vietnam are also practicing this method, but on a smaller scale.

However, no matter what method is used, the central point is that we must return to our true selves by being wordlessly aware of the present moment. When walking, doing exercises, waiting for the bus, eating, or drinking tea, we must constantly recognize the current conditions of our body and mind without ignoring reality. If we do not react by rejecting or grasping, but only follow (passively observe) the natural dynamics of the manifesting and vanishing of all phenomena, which operate according to the law of causes and conditions, we then will have a true and non-discriminating view of reality and a life full of freedom, selflessness, and altruism.

INSIGHT AND INNER CALM

Deep contemplation (Vipassana; insight) is one of the most important methods of practice for those who seek the path of liberation. The practice of insight enables people to change their perception, which is usually subjective and one-sided, and often merely a copy, an informed guess, or a hand-me-down of old knowledge. Insight shines a light on our body and mind and their present situation. By practicing deep insight, we clearly see the nature, form, and dynamic function of the interdependence of all phenomena, instead of sticking to erroneous perceptions about an independent self.

As the Buddha points out, the hiding or manifestation of all phenomena are the results of people's actions following the law of causes and conditions. In the Heart Sutra, the Tathagata taught about the insight that should be thoroughly understood by all practitioners:

"The Bodhisattva Avalokitesvara, while moving in the deep course of perfect understanding shed light on the Five Skandhas

(aggregates) and found them equally empty. After this penetration, he overcame ill-being." (*Plum Village Chanting and Recitation Book*)

Inner calm refers to a mind free from delusion, rejection, and grasping. Contemplation means looking deeply at reality without any intention of discrimination, any subjective perception of either like or dislike. Contemplation does not refer to a sitting position with half-closed eyes and thinking about distorting reality, fabricated by a self-based on desire. Contemplation is not waiting for an unwanted event to happen and then looking for a solution. Insight is letting go of all ambitions, aspirations, and cultivating a pure and empty mind. Insight is seeing reality as it is, as exemplified by a mere recognition of all bodily movements; when we walk, stand, and eat, we are aware that we are walking, standing, and eating. This deep contemplation enables us to live freely and at peace.

In the Four Foundations of Mindfulness Sutra, the Exalted One taught:

"Herein, Monks, a noble disciple lives contemplating the body in the body, ardent, clearly comprehending and mindful, having overcome covetousness and grief concerning the world. He lives contemplating the feeling in the feeling, ardent, clearly comprehending and mindful, having overcome covetousness and grief concerning the world. He lives contemplating the mental-states in the mental- states, ardent, clearly comprehending and mindful, having overcome covetousness and grief concerning the world. He lives contemplating the mental-objects in the mental-objects, ardent, clearly comprehending and mindful, having overcome covetousness and grief concerning the world." (*PTS: MN: Vol. I*)

Having insight into our body, feelings, mental states, and objects of mental states with diligence, understanding, and mindfulness does not refer to a separation of the subject and object, but to a mere recognition of reality. Contemplating the body in the body is simply recognizing its warm and cold, soft and hard states, the short or long in-breath and out-breath, without any intention of shaping or controlling them. The same method is applied to the contemplation of feelings, mental states, and objects of mind. If we are not controlled by the habits of grasping or resisting, discriminating and fabricating as programmed by the ego, then perfect wisdom (Prajnaparamita) will automatically manifest, and shine the light on the five aggregates – form, feelings, perceptions, mental formations, and consciousness – which turn out to be impermanent, without any independent self, and containing elements of suffering (in accordance with the Three Dharma Seals: suffering, impermanence, and no self.)

The Bodhisattva Avalokitesvara, upon recognizing the five aggregates as equally empty, overcomes ill being and attains liberation. Form manifests depending upon the combination of several elements which are continuously changing, as are feelings, perceptions, mental formations, and consciousness. They are not individual entities and must depend on each other to manifest. "Birth-death" and impermanence are facts of life. We cannot keep anything for ourselves and nothing lasts long enough for us to grasp onto it. Following such contemplation, anger, hatred, and delusion have no conditions for arising, and we will easily overcome pain and suffering, leading to a free and peaceful life.

This achievement is the essential nature and work of a Bodhisattva to bring benefit to yourself first, then you bring benefit to others.

Insight into inner calm is another translation of Avalokitesvara Bodhisattva. One of the deep meaning of Avalokitesvara is the capacity of deep and perfect listening. He listens to everything as it is without any judgment: thus, he overcomes all ill-being, and loves all sentient beings. Awareness, unification of mind, and wisdom are three essential conditions of a Bodhisattva's achievements.

Avalokitesvara has the power of listening to the sounds of the world and clearly understanding what arises in the body-mind in the present moment.

When our mind is not attached to anything, then we are able to hear the whispering going on in our mind. Such sounds are like sentient beings confined to the darkness of affliction and sorrow. Only Avalokitesvara Bodhisattva (awake awareness) can understand and transport these sentient beings (false perceptions) from the realm of delusion to the shore of enlightenment and happiness. If we practice this wordless awareness meditation, and always come back to ourself so we can listen to all the sounds in our mind – we can remain calm, realize the miracle of awakening to our true nature, and deeply and fully listen without interrupting others' words, regardless whether they be of praise or blame.

If we are impatient, we will never know all the unspeakable secrets of others. On the contrary, tranquility and clear seeing help us to observe reality as it is, without any sudden, mistaken reaction, and to realize that everything comes into existence due to favorable conditions. Even with diligent practice in order to end all afflictions and suffering and to reach peace and liberation, we still lack objective insight into their true nature. Therefore, insight into inner calm is to return inward to discover reality as it is and not as it may appear to be.

Everybody wants a happy life. Unfortunately, harmful habits of clinging to praise and rejecting blame, of seeing things with judgment or the intervention of our desires, often prevent people from enjoying a lasting happiness. Loving speech is beneficial to us and to others but becoming attached to it may bring more sorrow than joy. In reality, not everybody uses sincere loving speech, and human beings do have moments of rude or offensive behavior in their relations with others. We are no exception if we lack constant mindfulness in all our daily activities. Therefore, deep listening is very important in preserving happiness in our family and society.

To build good communication requires constant mindfulness of our thoughts, speech, and actions at any place and time. If our mind is as transparent as a mirror, then reality will be reflected objectively and accurately as it is. Thus, we will be free and serene anytime, anywhere, without attachment to anything. This is exactly the spirit of freedom and complete liberation of Avalokitesvara Bodhisattva when he dwells in perfect understanding of Emptiness.

BEING KIND TO EACH OTHER

All phenomena in life are changing from moment to moment. The human body-mind unceasingly goes through cycles of birth and death. Therefore, people who without opportunities to express gratitude toward benefactors or to be kind to their loved ones may live with regret and sorrow after they unexpectedly pass away. To avoid such regrets, we have to be kind to each other in the present moment rather promising to do so in the future.

Kindness is one of the important virtues necessary in improving relationships with friends and neighbors. It is based on our honest and reliable behavior which must be consistent from the beginning to the end of our life. Honesty and trust contribute to the reputation and success of a company, as well as the development of society.

These two virtues are also necessary for a lasting union of lovers. There are many cases where people's words and actions don't match. Sooner or later, their dishonesty and unreliable behavior will be revealed, and a broken relationship will eventually follow.

Modern society reflects obvious successful economic development but without parallel progress in spiritual life, resulting in severe deterioration of social ethics and moral values. Daily news reports the alarming rise of social vices including fraud, drugs addiction, and theft. Some even take advantage of people's trust to organize scams in temples. Trust is lost among people more and more making it much harder to do business and maintain trade agreements. These negative social factors create doubts, distrust, and defensiveness. As long as these negative aspects of society persist, everybody will live in insecurity and misery. Actually, thanks to deep contemplation, we realize that such deterioration in moral values is mainly due to the lack of mindfulness of community members. The Buddha compares the human mind to a monkey, and to a riderless a horse running wild. He also compared our human mind to a monkey swinging through the trees, grabbing one branch then letting it go only to seize another. Since our mind is easily distracted and incessantly changing, we must know how to tame it, otherwise our thoughts and actions will easily cause harm to society, as the Buddha teaches us:

"All phenomena have mind as their forerunner.
They have mind as their chief.
If one speaks or acts.
With a polluted mind
Suffering follows him
Just as the wheel follows the footprint of the ox."
"Mind precedes all states.
Mind is their chief.
They are all mind-wrought.
If a person speaks or acts
With a pure mind
Happiness follows him
Like his never-departing shadow."

(Dhammapada Verse 1 & 2)

Indeed, our speech and actions are always directed by our mind. If our mind is unwholesome and polluted, bad consequences will follow "like the wheel follows the footprint of the ox that draws the cart." On the contrary, if our mind is pure and clear, peace and happiness naturally manifest as "a never-departing shadow." Therefore, mind recognition and mind taming are the steppingstones for the development of our innate wisdom, which is the source of peace and happiness.

If we maintain a clear and objective view and know how to go with the flow of the law of causes and conditions, our mind will remain in stillness and purity. All phenomena work in the same way: we have to follow the flow, otherwise our ego will interfere and cause suffering. Our clear mind can help us to understand other people's behavior and lifestyle, and to express our empathy and love accordingly. Furthermore, our deliberate and calm attitude can abolish defensive thoughts or doubt, and allow better relations in our daily contact with others. Thus, happiness and positive social changes depend upon the kind behavior of each member of the community.

No one knows exactly how long we will live in this world. Human life is temporary and subject to unexpected events. It is a waste of time to maintain a defensive mentality reflecting distrust and anxiety, and not open our heart to living with others. Perhaps having experienced this feeling himself, the famous Vietnamese musician, Trinh Cong Sun, wrote these lyrics: "It's necessary to live with a heart. For what, do you know, darling? [It's a human need.], even for the wind to blow it away." (Let the Wind Blow), and "Life is not long, and we shouldn't be indifferent to each other." (From

Pink Rain) Vietnamese poet Ton Nu Hy Khuong also wrote: "Fame and fortune come and go like floating clouds; only love can last forever." (From Seeing Each Other)

There are families with abundant wealth and excess material comfort, but, unfortunately, parents and children, husbands and wives suffer from insecurity and lack of communication. Since they have spent too much time seeking fame and fortune, they no longer have time to listen deeply to each other and live fully with their loved ones. They do not realize that fame and fortune are illusions that "come and go like floating clouds," and only love remains. The only thing that we will carry along after our death are our thoughts and actions, also known as karma in Buddhist terminology. According to Buddha's teaching, our future life is the result of our own past actions. If our own actions and thoughts are wholesome in this life, we will be reborn in a good life; otherwise, it will be a life in the dark realm of pain and misery.

In fact, if we live a wholehearted life, we will be trusted, respected, and loved. Deep self-introspection is needed to fully get in touch with the present moment. A good example is when drinking a cup of tea, we must be fully aware of its taste along with our reaction in the moment. Thanks to this calm insight, we can see the true nature of life. This is also applying when we establish good relationships and are kind to each other. Awareness and mindfulness of the present moment will help us develop more understanding, cordial behavior, and an inherent inconceivable love, which are the necessary conditions for re-establishing peace, happiness, ethical values, security, and a prosperous society.

IN ACCORD WITH IMPERMANENCE

All things in this world are continuously changing including our human physical and mental state. Everyone should be aware of this process of change also called impermanence. This also means that nothing lasts forever. Everything exists over a short period of time and will be subject to transformation. Therefore, The Exalted One taught:

"All forms and phenomena are illusory" (Diamond Sutra)

"Form" in the Buddha's teachings does not simply refer to physical form but also includes the state of our mind. Actually, due to the impermanent nature of life, human beings are able to grow up, reach adulthood, and build up material assets. However, changes in life may cause suffering or happiness, depending upon each individual's perspective. If we go with the flow, conforming to the dynamics of nature without reacting, without following stereotypes or subjective perceptions, then no matter how things change, we still can enjoy the splendor of life.

Impermanence is a dynamic reality, continuously beginning anew like the flow of a river. Water and other elements in the universe depend on each other to manifest under different forms, including human life. Despite enormous differences, these elements always exist in accordance with conditions, without any separate self. Although they can change into multiple forms, they still adapt to all current circumstances as they are, unregulated by a self, wanting things to be as they "should be."

Human life undergoes endless changes. With time our body weight will change. Through education and social contact, a small child with simple knowledge grows up acquiring further intellectual capacity. Landscapes also change, as from an empty space into one crowded with high-rise buildings, or from a beautiful city back to a giant landfill after being destroyed by natural disasters. Thus, our body-mind and our circumstances always change. Nothing lasts forever as taught by the Exalted One in the Discourse on the Eight Realizations of the Great Beings:

"The First Realization is the awareness that the world is impermanent. Things composed of the four elements are empty, containing within them the seeds of suffering. Human beings are composed of Five Aggregates and are without a separate self. They are always in the process of change-constantly being born and constantly dying." (Plum Village Chanting and Recitation Book)

According to Buddhism, human beings are created from four elements – earth, water, air, and fire – along with the five aggregates of form, feeling, perception, mental formations and consciousness. When these cause and conditions end, they will transform into another form. The future life will be good or bad depending on behavior in the present moment. Having opportunities to learn from virtuous and wise masters helps people change their life to a wholesome one. On the other hand, in an unhealthy environment the unwholesome seeds within us will germinate and lead to a miserable life. Therefore, we must constantly contemplate the illusory and impermanent nature of phenomena and recognize the presence of "I" and "mine." Once our mind is clear, craving and grasping have no place to attach to, and there will be no possession or becoming.

We usually hope everything will happen according to our expectations. We feel happy when we get what we want, otherwise we suffer. Unfortunately, happiness only lasts for a short time. This limited view takes away our opportunities to enjoy the wonders of nature. Each season of a year has its own beauty, but if your mind is disturbed you will never be able to enjoy anything as the celebrated Vietnamese poet Nguyễn Du (1766–1820) expresses this in the following verses:

"What surrounding landscape wouldn't be tinged by your own gloom?
And when you feel desolate, how can what you see bring you joy?"

(The Tale of Kiều. Nguyễn Du).

Circumstances are continuously changing through the cycle of coming and going, being and non-being. The weather changes. Yet sunshine and rain each have their beauty. They are each necessary for life on earth; without either, sentient and non-sentient beings, including humans, animals, birds, plants and minerals, cannot exist. Grief and sorrow, stemming from a scattered and discriminative mind, along with a subjective perception of self, will obscure the true nature of all phenomena.

Indeed, sorrow and misery arise when we covet what we like or reject what we dislike. Meanwhile, all phenomena are operating according to the law of cause and effect, and are always changing beyond our capability to grasp. Thus, The Exalted One asked Rahula:

"What do you think about this, Rahula? Is the eye permanent or impermanent?"
"Impermanent, revered sir."
"But is what is impermanent, anguish or happiness?"
"Anguish, revered sir."
"But is it right to regard that which is impermanent, anguish, liable to alteration as, "This is mine, that I am, this is myself?"
"No, revered sir."

(PTS: MN, Vol. III: 147-329)

Impermanence clearly causes suffering, as people want to cling to "I" and "mine." If our view is not clear and our mind is scattered by ignorance or delusion, we cannot live in harmony with the law of impermanence and instead always want to keep what we like forever, hence suffering. All phenomena change not as we think they "are," nor as they "must be" according to some convention, nor as they "should be" as we wish. Due to impermanence, the illusory self will never be satisfied. Recognizing this truth, we can put an end to our false view, craving and grasping, and cease all anger, hatred, and delusion, which will lead to Nirvana where there is no self.

In short, conforming to the law of impermanence is to let go of the mind of craving and grasping. We do what needs to be done, and, once accomplished, let it go.

As such, our mind will be without likes or dislikes, free and tranquil, leading to peace and happiness.

FAMILY LEGACY

Some families have abundant material assets, excess food, expensive clothing, precious jewelry, but still cannot enjoy life, and whose children behave badly.

If the parents are not well educated and often argue or fight with each other, these unfavorable conditions will plant bad seeds in their children's mind and negatively influence their life later on. However, if parents set high moral standards based upon understanding and loving-kindness, then the children will inherit these noble values and continue to build upon the family legacy with their own strength.

Therefore, what needs to be transmitted to the next generation is not only material assets. More important is parental behavior that reflects purity and clarity.

In real life, many couples try tirelessly to make money, and don't pay enough attention to their children's education and outside activities. They think that money can buy everything and solve all their problems, so they entrust their children to the care of schoolteachers, ignoring the importance of basic family values. The children will then be spoiled and out of control, a burden to the family and the community.

Parents play a very important role in the mental development of intelligent and talented people who can contribute to the well-being of society. Lately, many people have studied and applied the 0-Years-of-Age program, founded by Feng De Quan. Professor Feng De Quan states, "From zero to six is the best age for the development of a child's nervous system and intelligence." Learning starts not only after childbirth but also during pregnancy. This concept of "fetal education" has been studied by many scientists from Israel, the United States, and China as well as several other countries. Many children raised in these experimental studies prove to be very smart and doing well at school. Viet Nam is also applying such popular international methods as The Montessori Method, The Schichida Method, and Glenn Doman's Achievement of Human Potential. In Hanoi, educational pioneer Lại Thị Hải Lý has founded the VSK (Vietnam Super Kids) Institute. Ms. Lại has organized many seminars and workshops on early education, guiding pregnant women on correct methods of child development.

"Fetal education" in fact refers also to the parents' education. If they do not behave kindly with each other and use loving speech, that will have an unwholesome effect on the fetus. In order to promote early child development, parents and loved ones must set examples of living in happiness with a pure, calm mind. In this way, we can clearly see the interconnection between parents and children, and ourselves and our environment— in other words, the interdependence of all things in the universe. Whether a child's life will be happy or unstable depends in part on the happiness or afflictions inherited from his or her parents. Therefore, a pregnant woman must be taken care of and cherished by her husband, brothers, sisters, and parents, whose positive behavior and peaceful energy greatly influence the baby's intelligence.

Parents must realize that every single word or action is an important lesson, constituting a stepping-stone for their children's future. Because a child's mind is as pure as a sheet of blank paper, parents write the first letters on it. There's a popular Vietnamese expression, "Parents give a child his body, but his character is god's work." The word "god" here is often misunderstood as referring to a sole supreme being. Instead, it refers to the influence of the whole society. From the Buddhist point of view, each individual's behavior is largely the result of his past karma; his parents and family members, not any god, are responsible for his education,

Actually, all things undergo changes, nothing remains the same, and everybody may have a good or bad attitude depending on his or her way of life in the present moment. Despite great knowledge and superior intelligence, if you are overconfident and lack the capacity for deep listening, patience, and calmness in order to share other people's thoughts, then your mind will be limited to narrow views based on rigid principles. To shine the light of wisdom, and to see the inter-connectivity of all phenomena, you must abandon the habit of grasping and learn to let go. In that way, your view will be independent of time or space, and will adapt easily to all conditions. Cultivating knowledge is not enough for enlightenment: you also need to practice deep contemplation to develop insight wisdom and overcome the three main afflictions of craving, anger, and delusion.

The development of wisdom is the most important task in human life, the Buddha teaches:

"Monks, just as the lion, the king of all animals, is considered supreme in the realm of animals in terms of strength, speed, and force – as such, monks, among the spiritual powers, the power of wisdom is supreme for Enlightenment." (SN: VI: 51. I. Sala (v, 227))

Buddha's teachings can be condensed into three main parts: discipline, awareness, and wisdom. Diligent practice of moral discipline and awareness will lead to wisdom, which is the strongest of all spiritual powers, comparable to the power of the lion, king of all the animals.

Thanks to wisdom, we know how to love appropriately and to live happily. There's a popular expression, "Perfect wisdom is a Buddhist's life profession." This means that a practitioner's supreme goal is to attain perfect wisdom. This is the only way to completely eradicate suffering and break the cycle of samsara.

To develop our inherent wisdom, we must be passively aware of our body and mind and present circumstances. When we stand, walk, sit, lie down, eat, get dressed, or wash dishes, we should simply recognize all our body movements without discrimination, grasping, or rejection. Wisdom as such immediately manifests. This awareness is not time consuming, nor does it interfere with our daily activities, and is of benefit without limit. Therefore, returning to present moment reality and gaining insight into our body-mind are necessary to improve our morality, and, at the same time, to help establish a firm moral foundation for our children. This is the essential substance of a family legacy to be carried forward to future generations.

THE BEAUTY OF ANGER

People usually react with anger when encountering an unwanted situation. An outburst of anger may cause harm to our body and mind, and instability to others. However, anger is only a temporary psychological state. It comes and goes in a short time. If we know how to maintain a calm, clear mind, we will discover several beautiful, good aspects of anger or sorrow.

Anger is a strong feeling of displeasure when the self cannot get what it covets. Anger is composed of several factors that arise in our mind. There is a misconception that anger or sorrow is created by external and objective conditions: if there is not a self (ego) with likes and dislikes, then who gets angry and towards whom?

Looking deeply, we see that anger, sorrow, and loneliness manifest along with the self of greed and also a wish for perfection. The nature of the self is to grasp after what it wants; if the self is unsatisfied, anger or sorrow will emerge. Everyone knows that anger creates suffering in oneself and causes harm to others, but still cannot avoid it. Perhaps, according to Buddhist teachings, the habits of anger and other emotions have been formed in our past lives; if so, the seeds of anger, complaint, blame, and sadness have been stored in all human beings. Some people get angry only for a moment, but quite a few others are obsessed and brutalized by anger for days. Greed, anger, and delusion, the three poisons in the human mind, are capable of nourishing unwholesome seeds, leading us to the samsaric cycle of birth and death, and endless suffering. Thus, anger is comparable to a small ember, that is capable of burning a forest.

The physiological effects of anger are multiple: breathlessness, skin turning either pale or red, heart arrhythmia, high blood pressure, and even heart attack or stroke. Social effects of anger include broken relationships between husband and wife, children and parents, other family members and friends, leading to separation, grief, and suffering. Occasionally, we do have regrets after a quarrel with family members and promise ourselves that such anger must not be repeated. However, as a Vietnamese proverb states, "A horse is acquainted with his old track," (equivalent to "Once a thief, always a thief"). Anger is already deeply rooted in our subconscious, and all it takes is just some offensive words from someone to trigger an immediate burst of anger beyond our mental/emotional control.

People try different methods of overcoming anger including drinking a lot of water, traveling for a few days out of town, and exercising to the point of exhaustion. In spite of any benefits from these methods, we still are unable to completely eliminate the roots of pain and anger. They are only temporary, like "using a stone to cover the grass"; once the stone is taken away, the grass will regrow. After the outburst of anger, it is evidently difficult to re-establish a warm relationship and good communication with our loved ones.

HAPPINESS: A MATTER OF PERSPECTIVE

Since each of us has an inherent capacity to transform greed and hatred, there is no need to look for it elsewhere but to simply look back into ourselves within the present moment. When we walk, we are aware that we are walking; when we sit, we are aware that we are sitting; the same for eating, and drinking. This practice of tacit awareness helps us confront unwanted situations with a calm mind and gently embrace them without avoiding, resisting, or rejecting anything.

All phenomena come and go, arise and pass away, following their own natural process of formation, without any negative intention of disturbing our mind. Since we want to select images, sounds, or situations to satisfy our passions and expectations, we are bound by the wanting self, and isolated from the world. Even an unreasonable situation may become an important lesson, enabling us to discover our ego (self). According to Buddhism, enlightenment and deliverance are only found when we identify and transform the craving and grasping self.

If we fully understand this Buddhist principle, all difficulties and obstacles including sorrow and anger, will become beneficial in our life, because benefit only manifests when our mind is tranquil and clear. For example, in a garden, instead of fully being present to enjoy the natural beauty of the flowers, we are dominated by the mind of choosing or grasping, which intervenes to distort reality. This greedy attitude robs us of our freedom, and prevents us from appreciating the beauty of the flowers as they are. Almost all of us fall into this kind of delusion by running after false happiness. Meanwhile, considering the dual aspects of life such as negative-positive, hot-cold, bright-dark, each aspect has its own beauty, so why must we always choose only one aspect? For instance, when looking at a flowerpot, it is unfair to only like the fragrant, beautiful upper growing part and reject the dirty lower part of dirt and decay, because if we cut off the roots, in only a few days the flowers will be transformed into rot.

With deep contemplation into impermanence in daily life, we can confront misfortune and humiliation like a cool breeze without worry or misery. Life is like a river of continuously flowing water. Nobody can grasp or covet anything. People who always want things to be as they wish never can see and enjoy true happiness.

A principle for transforming anger, hatred and delusion is to live with tacit awareness in the present moment. All our bodily functions and movements such as walking, standing, sitting, lying down, driving, washing, eating, drinking tea, or combing hair must be recognized with an objective view, as they are, without like or dislike, grasping or rejecting. Each person has his own karma, each life is shaped differently, and all actions must be carried out flexibly to accord with reality. Hastily looking for a way to abolish anger will unintentionally create more misery and confusion. Only a relaxed, letting-go mind is able to face all kinds of events in life, and enjoy them as easily as listening to a piece of soft music or looking at a beautiful natural landscape. This is the important practice for those who want to follow the Buddha's Path to attain Enlightenment and Liberation.

STAYING CAREFREE WHILE HAVING ATTACHMENTS

Human beings always long for a free, happy, peaceful life. To attain this goal, they work hard, make plans, and take on multiple projects. Yet many people don't achieve this goal. If our mind is dominated by ambitions for perfection, and refuses to accept unfavorable circumstances, freedom and peace will not be ours.

We are all connected to various people: family members, friends, and co-workers. These relationships create human bonds that involve love and hate, prejudice and covetousness. Parents will always protect their children, a husband sides with his wife, a big brother supports his younger brother. Our loved ones are always right and other people wrong. People use power and words to be on the winning side, even knowing their loved ones might have committed errors. But what happens if we are defeated in a dispute? Most likely we will become immersed in misery and may lose our power of self-control. To maintain our inner calm and freedom in such an entanglement of human connections requires constant contemplation into our body-mind and related circumstances in order to get beyond the chains of greed, hatred, and delusion.

Actually, we do not need to attain any particular goal to be happy. We also do not need to stay away from a difficult person to avoid trouble. But we do need to calmly face reality and recognize our self that craves and rejects. Our aspiration for perfection wastes energy and lessens the potential for enlightenment. The aspiration for leisure can be, in itself, the source of a dispersed and scattered mind. It might be compared to the scenario of a person who goes to the market and shouts: "Be quiet, everybody! Quiet!!" Other people will ignore him while he evidently is wasting his energy by only adding more noise to the crowd.

Meanwhile, we only need to recognize what is scattering our body-mind, while neither desiring nor resisting; then peace and happiness will manifest. The Tathagata Himself has realized this:

"Bhikkhus, when his mind is desiring, the practitioner is aware, 'My mind is desiring.' When his mind is not desiring, he is aware, 'My mind is not desiring.' When his mind is hating, the practitioner is aware, 'My mind is hating'. When his mind is not hating, he is aware, 'My mind is not hating.' When his mind is confused, the practitioner is aware, 'My mind is confused.' When his mind is not confused, he is aware, 'My mind is not confused.' When his mind is collecting, the practitioner is aware, 'My mind is collecting.' When his mind is not collecting, he is aware, 'My mind is not collecting.' when his mind is dispersed, the practitioner is aware, 'My mind is dispersed.' When his mind is not dispersed, he is aware, 'My mind is not dispersed.'

This is how the practitioner remains established in the observation of the mind in the mind; he remains established in the observation, free, not caught in any worldly consideration."

(Discourse on the Four Establishments of Mindfulness. Plum Village Chanting Book)

Phenomena in the universe are not bound together: they are interdependent, converging, and always changing. When proper conditions are met, clouds will change into rain, rivers, and streams; they change to another form when conditions are no longer favorable, but each element of the cloud still has its own individuality. Yet, since we live in mindlessness and delusion, we do not see clearly the nonself and dependent origination of all phenomena; therefore, we are controlled by the greedy, angry, and ignorant self, thence leading to preconception and confusion.

Meanwhile, as the Buddha taught, the true nature of all phenomena is inherently non-discriminating and free. So the above sutra affirms that we need merely to recognize the come-and-go nature of an emerging feeling, whether angry or joyful, without grasping or rejecting it. The habit of satisfying our senses (desire) and grasping what we like (craving) is the rope binding us to the cycle of Samsara of Six Realms. If the desiring self is not satisfied, sorrow and misery immediately arise, leading to conflict, struggle, and aversion (hatred). That is why the Buddha taught:

"Unstayed, friend, and unstriving did I cross the flood"
"But did thou, dear Sir, without stay, without striving, cross the flood"
"When I, friend, kept myself stayed, then verily
I sank; when I, friend, strove hard, then verily was I whirled about"
And so, friend, unstayed, unstriving did I cross the flood."
(PTS: SN: Part I: l. Crossing the Flood.)

"Stepping forward" means running after desires or ambitions, "staying" means grasping and coveting what we like. The Buddha's wisdom helps us see that both stepping forward or staying are each way of falling into the trap of greed and ignorance (delusion). A calm, and clear mind uncovers the benefit of the emerging anger, greed, and sorrow. Contemplating this truth, we will be able to let go of something's coming into being (possessiveness). We cannot use our will or reason to eradicate the thousand-year-old construction fabricated by the ego; instead, we only need to see clearly the dynamics of its formation, and then we will be able to leisurely stroll from the realm of birth and death to Nirvana.

Everyone wants to live with pleasant people and looks for favorable conditions to sustain their happiness. Not too many people can meet these expectations, because if our mind is mostly obsessed by craving and grasping, our view about people and society will be limited and one-sided. Furthermore, since we always want things to be "mine," when others covet the "mine" anger will emerge and cloud our inherently clear, pure, true mind. When our mind is subject to grief and anger, we are unable to appreciate the beauty of nature: mountains, dawn, birds fluttering in the front yard, innocent children frolicking in a sunny morning. The question is what can we do to attain freedom and happiness in this very life? The concern of "what can we do" reflects a scattered and impatient mind, dominated by a fabricating self. The answer is that we only need to see clearly how the disturbed mind arises and passes away, and simply recognize all body-mind activities as they appear. In other words, we must live with the flow, conforming to the law of causes and conditions, without resistance, rejection, or modification. Right in this moment, we attain freedom and inner calm.

In the process of releasing our fetters, and while pursuing a free and peaceful life, nothing is better than getting close to and learning from wise and virtuous masters. Their steady, calm energy will progressively shine light on our mind and enhance its clarity and purity. This is because staying free or getting attached is not caused by the outside circumstances but depends on each individual's perspective.

TWO ASPECTS OF LIFE

All phenomena in this world have a dual nature – win-lose, right-wrong, love-hate, beautiful-ugly, big-small, or hot-cold – which constitutes the essential nature of life. Each phenomenon exists in the other and vice versa. Looking deeply at a flower, we can see the presence of all the factors contributing to its formation, including fertilizers and garbage, and the reverse is true of future flowers being the present in a pile of garbage. Flowers and garbage are entities present within each other; one is needed for the existence of the other. They are not two but not one either. The reality is that by eliminating garbage, you will lose the beautiful flower. But not many people want to accept both sides of life. They only select the one conforming to their preference and may unintentionally lose both opportunities.

Human beings always try to possess the best things and attain everlasting happiness. Unfortunately, this aspiration is the source of emotions that can cause harm to the inherent happiness within each of us. A mind dominated by craving and grasping will lead to insecurity; even after being satisfied, one will still be subject to anxiety and the fear of loss. For example, after getting married to the one you love, you naturally wish to live with him or her forever, and try your best to treasure this love. If for some reason, he or she has an intimate relation with another person, he/she will suffer immensely. Therefore, the illusory ego first makes one suffer from craving, then from grasping and "becoming" (possession). By eliminating the concept of grasp-reject, we may attain true happiness. Human beings grow up with ordinary feelings of joy/sadness, love/hatred, and anybody without those feelings may be considered abnormal. So, it is almost impossible to reject the dual nature of all phenomena. It is better to contemplate and find the beauty in each phenomenon. Sorrow and anger have their own benefit; the important thing is to keep our calm to have deep insight and try to learn from them. To develop patience and great love, we have to go through good and bad times, the ups-and-downs in life.

Do you know why parents' love for their children is praised by writers and poets and compared to high mountains and vast oceans? Indeed, their sacrifices are immense; they have to work day and night, taking good care of the children, during pregnancy, after their birth, and throughout their adolescence. They spend time and energy for their education, which will contribute to the well-being of society. With such a noble task, they overcome all difficulties when encountering unwanted circumstances, from which they learn numerous practical lessons. So, if you try to avoid obstacles in life, your opportunity of understanding and love will be lost.

In reality, many people who live under favorable circumstances, with excessive material comfort, a happy family, a stable career, are not concerned about learning and practicing Dharma, about having a Dharma teacher; until they encounter bad luck, such as an accident, a serious illness, financial problems, or marital infidelity, then they feel empathy for other people's sufferings. From that moment, they try to take refuge in the Three Jewels, and diligently practice the Buddha's teachings, in order to acquire inner calm. Thanks to these unfortunate situations, one has the opportunity to wake up and turn toward the path of liberation, as expressed in Buddhist terms: "Affliction is Bodhi." (Affliction is inseparable from Awakening.) Affliction and Buddha nature are considered two sides of the same coin.

If you are strongly determined to build up a healthy and happy way of life for you and your loved ones, this favorable energy will provide you with the power to surmount craving, anger, and grasping. The Exalted One has taught:

"Monks, there are these two powers. What two? The power of computation and the power of cultivation."

"And what, monks, is the power of computation? Herein a certain one just reflects: Evil is the fruit of immorality in body, both in this life and in the life to come. Evil is the fruit of immorality in speech, both in this life and in the life to come. Evil is the fruit of immorality in thought, both in this life and in the life to come."

"Thus reflecting he abandons immorality of deed in body, speech and thought, and cultivates morality therein, and so conducts himself in utter purity. This, monks, is called the power of computation."

"And what, monks, is the power of cultivation? In this case the power of cultivation pertains to those under training. By virtue of the power of training, monks, he abandons lust, abandons hatred, and abandons delusion. So doing, he does no ill deed, he pursues not wickedness. This, monks, is called the power of cultivation."
(PTS: AN: Vol. I; Chapter II; 1-10. Disputes)

If you constantly apply ethics, awareness, and contemplation in every action, speech or thought in the present moment, you will not harm yourself and others nor create unwholesome consequences in this life and future lives. This is called the power of computation. On the other hand, once your mind is truly clear and calm, the ego of craving, grasping and delusion cannot affect your life. At that moment, all bad actions will stop, and you are completely free and liberated right in this life. This is called the power of cultivation that all practitioners employ.

To adjust our perception and misbehavior, we must follow the Buddha's teachings:

"Bhikkhus, when his mind is desiring, the practitioner is aware, 'My mind is desiring.' When his mind is not desiring, he is aware, 'My mind is not desiring.' He practices in the same way concerning a hating mind, a confused mind, a collected mind, a dispersed mind, an expansive mind, a narrow mind, the highest mind, and a concentrated and liberated mind." (Sutra on the Four Establishments of Mindfulness)

If during meditation, your mind is scattered and you urgently want to eliminate your disorganized thoughts, then you are not meditating anymore. The attitude of looking for calmness is, in itself, the cause of insecurity. But quite a few people who like to "avoid the troubled world and look for the quiet one" are misled, controlled by craving, anger, and delusion. The passage from the above sutra shows that when a thought, even a good one arises in your mind, you only need to fully recognize it as it is, without any like or dislike, then your "self" will vanish. Thanks to this practice, the bhikkhu finds the operation dynamics of birth-death of all phenomena, and no longer wants to possess and grasp anything in life.

To better understand the true meaning of life, we must come back to ourselves and constantly observe our body and mind and related circumstances. Wherever you are, whatever you do, always keep practicing this way, so that your body and mind come to a state of pure and calm unity. Your view of the world will not be affected by the discriminating of one side over the other. Instead, you will treasure life with loving-kindness.

COME AND SEE

During a conversation with friends, you may have talked about an ideal, peaceful place, and dreamed of visiting it, to see it with your own eyes. Then news and media images might intensify your imagination of this place, which becomes more and more attractive to you. However, when you have a chance to see for yourself, to spend time and share some activities with people who live there, you recognize the difference between the real world and the one you'd been dreaming of. You might then realize that your idealized view is always limited. Only by getting in touch with current circumstances can you see reality as it is, clearly and not as in your erroneous imagination.

Quite a few people like to idolize a famous person or organization and, in so doing, give up their own inherently objective and truthful view. Perhaps they become accustomed to comparison and prejudice, prefabricated by their own ego; yet, even after recognizing some unwholesome and negative aspects of their idol, their mind is still dominated by a perfect image and ideal and are limited to a superficial and simplistic view of every phenomenon, Therefore, they lose the chance to learn from other people and organizations and miss out on getting valuable lessons that can help them analyze and understand thoroughly the problems of they're concerned with. If a concept or principle, based on some stereotype, has formed in your mind, you may easily lose your freedom and potential power of liberation. The path to enlightenment means not getting attached to any concept or doctrine, even the noble aspiration of attaining Buddhahood.

On the other hand, you may become disappointed when faced with reality, when it differs too much from information given to you by your friends or the media. To avoid this, it is best to recognize both the negative and positive sides in every person or situation.

In fact, it is impossible to find an ideal place where there is no negative manifestation, unless people are completely free from greed, anger, and delusion. If you do not recognize these negative feelings when they arise, you will be controlled by subjective and one-sided opinions, causing suffering in yourself and others. This is what the Buddha taught:

"Brahmin, one who is ablaze with lust, overwhelmed with lust, infatuated thereby, plans to his own hindrance, to that of others, to the hindrance both of self and others, and experiences mental suffering and dejection. If lust be abandoned, he no longer plans thus, no longer suffers thus. So far, Brahmin, Dharma is seen in this life, it is a thing not involving time, inviting one to come and see, leading onwards, to be realized for themselves by the wise." (PTS: AN: Vol I; Part III: 53. The Brahmin)

The main point is, when the desiring mind arises and brings no benefit, or the mind free of greed arises and leads to happiness, you clearly recognize these arising and passing away states of mind as clearly as when you observe birds fluttering in your front yard in an early morning. You simply recognize this phenomenon of coming and going without the intervention of your desiring self or rejecting self; otherwise, you will be bound by a chain of negative emotions, such as sorrow, anxiety, grief, worry and so forth.

Therefore, the above sutra indicates that "Dharma is seen in this life ... not involving time, inviting one to come and see." Sometimes, you may come to see that ideal person and you are present with him under the same conditions, but you still cannot find any real meaning to life! So where are we going? If there were a real point of arrival in time and space, there would be also an end point. But in reality, all things have no beginning and no ending, without place or location as conventionally perceived; all phenomena are equal without any discrimination. Therefore, "come and see" means to come back to yourself, to the here and now in order to see that all things in the universe are like a flowing river, and see them as they are, without adding any judgment. When the true nature of a phenomenon is manifesting, you will be able to see the substance, the characteristics, and the function of everything. By understanding the inter-connectedness of all things in life, including your own true nature, you have no more desire to possess anything instead, you are capable of "leading onwards; to be realized for themselves by the wise."

This is pure truth, but most of the time, we live in illusion, following our imagination and not living in harmony with the current situation. A good example is if you are used to getting scared and running away when seeing a snake. This fear goes deep into your subconscious, so that the next scenario is that, in dim light, you may mistake a rope for a snake. Your view is always influenced by your past experiences or a prefabricated stereotype. Just as if you're seeing the world through colored glasses: you simply need to remove the glasses and truth will appear. Without intervention of your subjective judgment, you will get in touch with the reality as it is. Life is a dynamic process, always changing moment to moment and beginning anew. If your mind is not clear and clever, you will feel isolated like a cell separated from the body.

Nowadays, we live in a fast-paced, busy society. Pressures of work have a strong influence on our mind, which may lead to stress and even depression. Regardless of their material possessions, mental illness will definitely prevent people from living in peace and happiness. Therefore, besides working for a living, we'd best invest our time in Dharma practice to stabilize and purify our mind and develop wisdom.

Today, not only in Vietnam, people in the materially developed countries of Europe, America, and Australia study, investigate, and apply Buddha's teachings in daily life. As Buddhist philosophy is very realistic and shares many commonalities with modern science, employees of such famous high-tech companies as Google, Facebook and Apple have begun to practice meditation in order to be free of worry, to de-stress and find balance in their lives.

In short, to practice the Buddha's teachings is to find peace and happiness, contributing to the security and prosperity of one's society and country. In any place and at any moment, we return to reality, and objectively recognize our body-mind-circumstance as it is. We are aware of what we are doing. When body and mind come together as one, wherever or whenever we come or go, our view no longer depends on circumstances of time or space; then the hearing is only the hearing, the seeing is only the seeing.

Afterword by Dr. Mylene Tran Huynh

I first heard Bhikkhu Thich Vien Ngo speak a few years ago at a Sunday service at Hoa Nghiem Pagoda in Fort Belvoir, Virginia. I was captivated by the depth and clarity of his explanation of Buddha Dharma in layman's terms. Through heartfelt stories and gentle humor, his insightful sermons always leave a deep impression in my heart as I yearn to apply his teaching. Eventually, I had the honor of meeting him and received his gift of guidance in *Happiness: A matter of perspective*.

In this book, Bhikkhu Thich Vien Ngo masterfully blends Buddhist wisdom with Vietnamese cultural traditions to give us practical tips akin to modern psychology as a means to achieving lasting happiness. Through astute anecdotes and doctrinal accounts, he engages the reader by connecting daily encounters with ancient teachings. He shares the secrets of living a prosperous and happy life through inner reflections, self-observations, and intentional expression of suitable responses. In the first chapter, he challenges us to boldly face our sufferings head-on. He advises us to embrace life's difficulties as precious teachers, and encourages us to listen and look deeply to understand others. For when we understand another being, we cannot help but love her.

Afterword by Dr. Mylene Tran Huynh

I appreciate the relevance and ease of applying Bhikkhu Thich Vien Ngo's teachings in my daily life. One of my favorites is when he suggests we should live like our hands." As a physician who also practices acupuncture, I am beholden to my hands for what they can accomplish, never tiring and never complaining Whether I am examining a patient, grooming the garden or washing the dishes, my hands are always perfectly synchronized with present moment without lingering in the past or anticipating the uncertain future. As I watch my hands type these words, I am in a state of grateful presence. I strive to live like my mindful hands.

The essence of Bhikkhu Thich Vien Ngo's teachings is, in fact, rooted in mindfulness. In recent years, medical science has recognized that mindfulness meditation stimulates positive physical and functional changes in the brain. Clarity and awareness brought about through meditation decrease stress, improve moods, enhance focus, and maximize performance. Today, such leading-edge medical treatments as Acceptance and Commitment Therapy combine mindfulness with psychotherapy to facilitate self-awareness, acceptance, and responsible action through insight and proper view.

Bhikkhu Thich Vien Ngo tells us that true happiness begins with connecting with our True Self to awaken our inner light, which can shine with brilliance when we pause to connect with our Mind and gain clarity of perspective. We all possess that internal flame, capable of magnificent radiance through time-tested guidance.

Thank you, Bhikkhu Thich Vien Ngo, for the gift of wisdom that empowers us to live a life full of present moments and to act from an open and compassionate heart.

Thank you, Dr. Ton That Chieu, for translating these eloquent teachings into English so that many people can discover true happiness.

Enjoy the transformational journey as you apply the lessons!

In gratitude,

Mylene Tran Huynh, MD, MPH

McLean, Virginia

Translator's Note

Translating *Hạnh Phúc Tùy Cách Nhìn* (*Happiness: A matter of perspective*) into English has made me all the more grateful to the Buddha's teachings. It is such a great lesson that human beings can find peace and happiness by simply looking more deeply into reality as it is.

From a humble intent to help beginners in Buddhist studies who cannot read Vietnamese but are interested in reading this book, I have tried my best to engage in the art of translation. Actually, if it hadn't been for the encouragement from its author, Dharma teacher Bhikkhu Thich Vien Ngo, and my Dharma friends at the Mindfulness Sangha of the Hoa Nghiêm Temple, I wouldn't have dared to assume the task.

From the first day I confided to my wife, Nguyen Khanh Bui Boi Tien, that I wanted to translate this book, despite her hesitation, she has offered steadfast support in the translation. I am grateful to her for her dedication and understanding.

A serious scholar of Vietnamese and American literature, my friend Tran Lac Dao was very helpful in translating several verses and proverbs in this book. My heartfelt thanks to him.

A few chapters have been edited by Ton and Bao Chau; I appreciate their patience and time.

My appreciation and thanks also go to Andrew Webbink for his time and effort in editing and proofreading the translation.

Last but not least, I would like to extend my appreciation to those who will read this book. And if readers find any benefits from reading this translation, then I feel very happy to have done something meaningful as an offering to the Temple and to the Three Jewels.

Ton That Chieu, MD (Tam Hien)

Sponsoring Member, Pali Text Society Bethesda, Maryland

Glossary

Arahant: A "worthy one"; one who has eliminated all defilements and attained full liberation in this life.

Bhikkhu: A Buddhist monk. (A nun is a bhikkhuni.) The word in Sanskrit/Pali means Literally means literally means "beggar" or "one who lives by alms"; a mendicant. "One who has transcended both good and evil; who follows the whole code of morality; who lives with understanding in this world, is indeed called a bhikkhu." (Dhammapada 267)

Bodhisattva: A future Buddha; an enlightened being who defers full Buddhahood in dedication to helping others cross the stream of birth and death and attain liberation.

Brahma: A supreme deity who rules over the brahma world; a class of superior devas inhabits the form realm.

Causes and conditions: Nothing exists independently, but, rather, comes into existence only in dependence upon various previous causes and conditions. Phenomena arise and pass away depending on causes and conditions.

Deva: A deity or God inhabiting heavenly worlds.

Dharma: The cosmic principle of truth, lawfulness, and virtue taught by the Buddha. It also includes all phenomena, things, and manifestations of reality. Since all phenomena are subject to the law of causation, this fundamental truth comprises the core of the Buddha's teachings.

The Five Precepts: The ethical code of Buddhism,

consisting of nonharm, not stealing, sexual propriety, truthfulness, and sobriety.

The Five Skandhas: Form, feelings, perceptions, mental formations, and consciousness. Upon examination, they are each found to be without intrinsic reality.

Karma: A Sanskrit word meaning an action and a reaction; the continuing process of cause and effect.

Maitreya: A Bodhisattva due to become the Buddha of the next era.

Nirvana: The final goal of the Buddha's teaching; a state to be attained by the destruction of all defilements.

Samsara: The round of rebirths without discoverable beginning, sustained by ignorance and craving.

Sangha: The monastic spiritual community.

Tathāgata: The epithet the Buddha uses most often to refer to Himself. The original meaning of the word might mean "one who has thus gone" or "one who has thus come." One interpretation is that it signifies that the Tathāgata has transcended the human condition, beyond all coming and going.

The Three Poisons: In Buddhist teachings, anger, greed, and ignorance are at the root of suffering. They are termed poisons because their influence is toxic. Each can be known by other names – such as aversion, attachment, and delusion – but they each are to be recognized, understood, and transformed.

Uposatha: The Buddhist observance days when the monks gather to recite the precepts.

Comments on HAPPINESS: A MATTER OF PERSPECTIVE

By Thích Không Triệt (David B. Johnson, Ph.D.)

This book discusses the various aspects of worldly happiness and that it is one side of the happiness/sadness dichotomy. It shows us how we can realize a state of ultimate happiness (equanimity/serenity/peace) through our understanding of the Buddha Dharma and through various Buddhist practices that help us transcend worldly happiness.

This is a good book for the experienced Buddhist to refresh their practice as well as those who are just beginning to learn about and/or practice Buddhism.

By Viên Đạo (JD White)

So wonderfully clear and directly accessible, *Happiness: A Matter of Perspective* is written with care and compassion. Thích Viên Ngộ suggests how we, all of us, can skillfully invite the Dharma to walk at our side and how we can act mindfully from the heart of our true home.

About the Author

Born in Quảng Trị Province, Vietnam, 1975, Venerable Thích Viên Ngộ entered the monastic order in 2000 at the Phước Viên Buddhist Temple in Biên Hòa, Đồng Nai Province, Vietnam. He joined Bát Nhã Monastery, Bảo Lộc Lâm Đồng Province from 2006 to 2008 to study with Zen Master Thích Nhất Hạnh. After that, he learned the Trúc Lâm Zen at Tue Quang Monastery for one year. He then studied with The Most Venerable Viên Minh, a Vipassana Buddhist Master from the Theravada tradition, from 2010 to 2012, at Bửu Long Temple, Ho Chi Minh City, Vietnam. He earned his Diploma in Buddhist Studies (2012) at Buddhist College and took Temple Abbot Training, and Dharma Teacher's Proficiency.

In addition to *Happiness - A Matter of Perspective* (2012, Vietnamese), he was a staff writer for the Vietnamese-language Giác Ngộ Buddhist Magazine from 2009 to 2012 in Ho Chi Minh City. While there he also wrote Mindful Manners for Lay Practitioners and Daily Buddhist Recitations.

Since 2013, he has been in the Washington, D.C. metropolitan area teaching meditation and providing counsel to people from all walks of life. Currently, he is the Abbot of Đạo Viên Monastery in Edgewood, Maryland.

Home page: *www.tuviendaovien.com*